EXTREME
Forgiveness

PRAISE FOR *EXTREME FORGIVENESS*

"Attorney Bob Crathorne was a key member of our Law Department before he was lost in the sinking of the USS *Maddox* during World War II. Now Bruce Frazer has done a marvelous job telling us the important details through his interviews with Luftwaffe pilot Dr. Kurt Fox, whose bomber crew sank the *Maddox*."

—THOMAS MacLEAY, CHAIRMAN, PRESIDENT & CEO, NATIONAL LIFE GROUP

EXTREME
Forgiveness

BRUCE W. FRAZER & CAROL E. GLASGOW

EDUCATOR'S INTERNATIONAL PRESS
Kingston, New York

Cover design by Richard Hendel
Page design and typesetting by Pratt Brothers Composition

Dedicated to Jeline Hinkson and her family, who personified extreme forgiveness when they looked into the eyes of the man who had murdered the family patriarch . . . and forgave him.

CONTENTS

CONTENTS

PROLOGUE

A lifetime of medical emergencies as a country doctor conditioned Kurt Fox to think and act fast. His one word greeting when he answered the phone, "Fox," encouraged callers to get right to the point. Nothing had prepared him, however, for a totally unexpected phone caller on January 15, 1995, who asked about his activities on July 10, 1943. This instantly took him back fifty-two years to a dark night at the beginning of the Allied invasion of Sicily during World War II (WWII). With 3,200 ships, 4,000 aircraft, and 250,000 troops, this was the largest Allied invasion to date. Kurt Fox was not among them; he was flying a Ju 88 dive bomber for the Luftwaffe, and his objective that night was to sink allied ships.

One of his bombs scored a direct hit on depth charges carried by USS Maddox (DD-622), which broke in two and, in just ninety seconds, sank, carrying with it 210 officers and men to the bottom of the Mediterranean. Seventy-four crewmembers survived. Kurt and his crew knew they had scored a hit but did not know the name of the ship or the extent of the damage or casualties. These specifics were confirmed during this surprise phone call, which was from a military historian who was in contact with the Maddox survivors group.

This book is about Kurt Fox's thoughts and actions from childhood through his service in the Luftwaffe and, after the war, his training as a physician who immigrated to America, where he served as a beloved country doctor for twenty-nine years. Most importantly, it tells of his poignant meeting with USS Maddox survivors who inducted him into their organization as an honorary member.

It is truly a story of extreme forgiveness.

ACKNOWLEDGMENTS

This little book with a big message was written with help from caring friends. We especially thank:

Chris Fox
Brian Lindner
Les Querry
John Schmid

"Am I not destroying my enemies
when I make friends of them?"

ABRAHAM LINCOLN

PREFACE

The circumstances under which my wife Carol and I meet interesting military veterans and aviation notables have always amazed us. Consider for example, Dr. Kurt Fox, who flew dive bombers for the Luftwaffe, then immigrated to America after earning his medical degree in Munich. He became a much admired country doctor who practiced for twenty-nine years in Fairfield, Virginia, after which he volunteered to provide medical assistance at two Indian reservations.

We had heard about this amazing fellow through our mutual friend, Les Querry, an Air Force Academy alumnus with an avid interest in aviation. Les had recently married my wife's cousin Marty, and he introduced Carol and me to Kurt at the wedding reception in Bluemont, Virginia on June 17, 2000.

Our meeting with Dr. Fox was celebratory and certainly a lot of fun: it was held in a children's petting zoo at a country vegetable farm!

Music from a dulcimer band, coupled with Dr. Fox's German accent, made it difficult for me to catch every word, but I heard enough to realize this was someone I wanted to know better and perhaps write about.

I have always been interested in forgiveness and reconciliation phenomena which Dr. Fox and many of his former American enemies must have experienced. What enabled these one-time mortal enemies to forgive and be forgiven? Was it simply the passing of time? Similar or differing cultures? Spirituality? Only the story of Kurt's life, along with observations of those who knew him best, would tell the full story.

Carol and I interviewed Dr. Fox twice in his retirement condominium in Charlottesville, Virginia, late in 2000 and early in 2001. I had hoped to place an abbreviated version of our interview in one of the aviation magazines that had carried my articles. Understandably, the chaos and disruptions of 9/11 made our publishing friends wary about running articles about wars, past or underway. Then, recently, we re-read the transcript and realized it had the makings of this book.

"Everyone says forgiveness is a lovely idea, until they have something to forgive...."

C.S. LEWIS

EXTREME
Forgiveness

WHEN AND WHERE

Carol and I recorded our interviews with Dr. Fox. Our questions and his answers that follow are very nearly verbatim and he edited the transcript.

FRAZER. After the amenities, I mentioned to Dr. Fox that I had lots of questions, the first of which was when and where he was born and why he had such a seemingly non-Germanic name.

DR. FOX. I was born February 26, 1922, in Bischofstein, East Prussia. It was a part of Germany like an island cut off by the Polish Corridor established by the Versailles Treaty, so we were a little bit isolated. The area was German for 700 years. Teutonic Knights started colonization in 1230, and East Prussia was a bit like the California of Germany. It was settled by many different German tribes.

The Teutonic Knights pushed out the original Pruzzen population, which was probably more Slavic than Germanic.

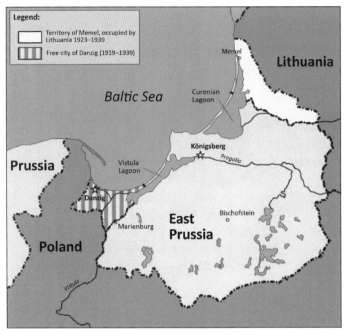

Legend:
Territory of Memel, occupied by Lithuania 1923–1939
Free city of Danzig (1919–1939)

Lithuania
Memel
Baltic Sea
Curonian Lagoon
Königsberg
Pregolia
Prussia
Vistula Lagoon
Danzig
Bischofstein
Marienburg
East Prussia
Poland
Vistula

East Prussia as determined by the Versailles Treaty, 1919–1939. Courtesy John Schmid

Anyway, you could find many names and many tribes in East Prussia. The fact that I have an English name was explained to me by a professor from Washington and Lee University who found out that, in the eighteenth century, the king of Poland, Augustus the Strong, imported 30,000 Scotch-Irish mercenaries to fight for him. Many of these people never left. East Prussia was the only area in Germany where you found English names; we had von Williams and Simpsons, and the banker across the street was O'Rourke! So, Fox wasn't such an unusual name in the area.

East Prussia (also known as Prusse Orientale), where Dr. Fox was born and grew up, was " . . . like an island cut off on the East." So he and his family felt "a little bit isolated." Small wonder!

The Fox family initially lived in Bischofstein (now Bisztynek). They later moved to Marienburg in the southwest quadrant.

Germany overran the Polish Corridor in 1939. After WWII, the region was placed under Polish administration and "ethnically cleansed" according to the post-war Potsdam Agreement. The native population was expelled and replaced with Poles. However, most Germans had already fled westward to avoid the Russian onslaught.

GROWING UP IN THE FOX FAMILY

FRAZER. So according to your Washington and Lee professor friend, your DNA probably shows a link to Scotch-Irish mercenaries. But what of your family in recent times?

DR. FOX. My father was a country doctor all his life. He was wounded in World War I (WWI) and wounded again near Warsaw in the first weeks of World War II. He had twenty grenade splinters in his right leg for the rest of his life and continued to practice all through the war in Marienburg in East Prussia. But before the Russian occupation, he escaped by ship from Danzig to Rostock in Mecklenburg and settled north of Berlin, which, unfortunately, later became the Soviet occupation zone. He continued his practice until he died in 1960.

The son of small farmers, my father was the only one in his family who went to university. His oldest brother got the farm, which was only four kilometers from where I was born, and he eventually was shot and killed by the Russians when they moved in in 1945. His wife survived.

My mother was the daughter of a *Gutsbesitzen* rancher [a large ranch] that had its own name in East Prussia. So she came from a nice background and I knew my grandparents on my mother's side very well. My grandfather died in 1931 at age sixty-three, when I was nine. He was the first dead person I ever saw. We had a very good relationship and I was his favorite grandson. I spent many of my vacations on their farm. And I have only good memories about that time.

FRAZER. I too spent time on a farm and loved every minute of it. What did you like most about it?

DR. FOX. Oh, I liked horses. I still like them. And it was a big, free life. The farm employed eight families; we had about seventy holstein cattle and produced milk and everything else. And there were seventy acres of woods and a lake. My time with the kids of the farm workers was a very happy time. We organized teams and we played and we raced the horses.

FRAZER. Did you help with the chores?

DR. FOX. Not really, I was too young. As grandson of the owner, there was a tremendous gap. People who worked there had a little land and house with one cow and had two or three pigs and they got paid on top of it. But there was a tremendous social difference. These kids, for instance, never came into the house where I was. But we played and I'd have lunch with them. I took my family there in 1972 and it's completely run-down. There's no house or the stable that used to house twenty or so horses—it's all gone. The Poles have not kept it up.

EARLY EDUCATION

AUTHOR'S NOTE. Looking ahead—Dr. and the future Mrs. Fox would have three children and three members of this incredible family would win Fulbright Scholarships! Now, back to the present . . .

FRAZER. You are obviously well educated, and it's apparent that a German education, at least in the early stages, is markedly different from what Americans are accustomed to. Please tell us why.

DR. FOX. I went to a normal public school, but schools in Germany were, and still are to a certain degree, different than in America. At age ten, children switch to a higher education track that prepares them for a university, or they remain in a curriculum which is more vocationally oriented and does not necessarily prepare them for a university. There are nevertheless alternatives that allow these "practically

11

trained" students to attend universities if they decide to do so later in life.

With my parents' encouragement, I chose to pursue a university education. This meant attending a very old-fashioned gymnasium, which is very different than American athletic gymnasiums. As gymnasium students, we received a humanistic and old-fashioned classical education; I had eight years of Latin, five years of Greek, and four years of French. English was for girls only, which didn't help me much when I eventually immigrated to the States. I graduated from the school my father had attended, and I even had a Latin teacher who still knew him. It was an old Jesuit school which, because of a lack of enough Jesuits, later on became just a Catholic high school. It was all very conservative.

I had a brother three years younger than I born in 1925, as well as a sister born in 1928, and their school experiences were similar to mine.

The area in which we lived in East Prussia, the so-called Ermland, was a small, historically grounded, island of Catholicism. When the Teutonic Knights converted to Protestantism, this little four-county area was under the dominance of the king of Poland, who was Catholic, and its inhabitants escaped the conversion to Protestantism. Catholicism remained dominant for almost 500 years.

I finished high school in 1938 and our family moved to Marienburg, a very nice city with a beautiful castle, the seat of the high master of the Teutonic Knights.

My father was a doctor, and it seemed logical for me to follow in his footsteps. So, to further my education, I registered as a medical student at Medical Academy in Danzig. It was the only medical academy in Germany; all the other

Kurt Fox, age circa seventeen

medical schools were universities. But since Danzig was a territory of the League of Nations, it was administered separately until January 1940.

To prove I had requisite qualifications as a student I needed an Abitur signified by a little card the size of a driver's license. It showed I was enrolled as a medical student and it was honored throughout Germany. Only ten to fifteen percent of all young people qualified. It was a rigorous curriculum: eight years of Latin, five years of Greek, four years of French. I had all this by age seventeen and a certificate to prove it. If anyone asked what I did as a civilian, I'd just say I was a medical student.

STORM CLOUDS

FRAZER. It seems that at least part of your life—through a good part of the '30s—was sort of bucolic. Was it?

DR. FOX. Well, yes in many ways, but, looking back, many were in denial or so it seemed. It all started very innocuously. It had been a depressed time, and within a year, there was no unemployment anymore, the people were doing fine, and everybody was quite optimistic.

In the beginning, economics was important, no question about it. Even to the people who were very skeptical, my father in the Deutsche National party, former officers, and upper class industrialists, Hitler was a little sergeant; he was nothing. He had no social standing, but his initial successes, came one after another in a short time. This quieted many of his critics. No one could have imagined the Nazis would kill six million Jews.

The two chancellors before Hitler, both appointed by President Hindenburg, were Franz von Papen, who was later exonerated in the Nuremberg trials, and a former general, Kurt von Schleicher, who resigned and was later executed. Hindenburg was certainly more to the right than the left, and for him to give communists power in Germany was unthinkable.

Other parties, especially the Deutsche National, the right wing, hated Hitler, but feared a communist take-over. Although the Nazis had a plurality in the 1932 elections, they did not have a majority. Nevertheless, opposition groups were unable to come together to form a majority coalition, and they reasoned they had no choice but to go with Hitler—he had the biggest party and coalition in the Reichstag, and Hindenburg had to appoint him chancellor.

FRAZER. This helps explain why the German nation was saddled by the Nazi party; these are reasons, not excuses. They don't explain what triggered the genocide or ruthless takeover of Poland and beyond. What were the most notable effects of all of this on you and your family with the passage of time?

DR. FOX. It was—how should I say—innocuous. It didn't hurt you personally. A lot of the things the Nazis pushed seemed compatible with established traditions. One little thing I'll always remember. In our small town, there were three doctors and my father had built a nice house—it's still there, it's now a Polish clinic.

My father never accepted the Weimar Republic flag, the present German flag, black, red and gold. He flew the black, red, and white old Imperial German flag. So we had a pole in our yard and, on certain holidays, I had to pull up the flag. So I remember my class comrades stood behind the fence and threw stones at me. Everybody in town knew who was a communist, Nazi (National Socialist German Workers' Party), or "Sozi" (Social Democrat). Nevertheless, we played soccer together!

The nationalistic part of the Nazi regime attracted people very much. Of course, when the war started, people, especially those who fought in WWI, had their doubts. They were quite worried from the beginning. But then again, Poland in twenty days, France soon thereafter, how do you fight that?

When the Hitler Youth started it was scarcely noticeable in our little East Prussian town. But two or three years later, every child in the school was involved. We were called *Jungenvolk* to age fourteen and from fiftee to eighteen we were in Hitler Youth. Then, above eighteen, there were other organizations. So it was a pretty automatic process. Oh, there was some resistance indirectly; this was a very Catholic town, with Catholic youth organizations. But even those people joined. There was really no way around it. You couldn't stay out and say, "I'm not going."

"When you forgive, you in no way change the past—but you sure do change the future."

BERNARD MELTZER

THE HEEL COMES DOWN

FRAZER. What were the penalties for "staying out"?

DR. FOX. Oh, for young people? You would be ostracized more or less—you would have difficulties. Even your school work would be looked at differently. You would be disadvantaged—you couldn't do this or you couldn't do that. Even if you had a very strong religious affiliation or political reason, it didn't count anymore because there was no political body to back you or for which you could have said "I belong to this or that."

There was only one party and if you stayed out of that as a young person and went into some sort of apprenticeship, that part of your life was completely involved in the system—however, I went to school until I was eighteen. In the beginning, as long as you played along, there was no problem. You would have to belong to a rare religious sect or your parents would have to be avid communists.

Unions, which were originally social democrats, went into the *Arbeitsfront*, the Nazi organization of unions, within three months. There were simply no more unions and many of the unions we have in America came from German unions we had around the turn of the century.

It's hard to describe; you have to live in a thing like this. Of course, the Germans are probably more authority-loving and disciplined and if they decide everybody has to do it then everybody does it. You have to realize afterward, things look quite different. But in the beginning, when you get into something like this, you cannot judge the consequences. There has never been anything like this in history.

FRAZER. You say that, at first, penalties for not going along were fairly nominal. At what point and how did things change?

DR. FOX. Hitler had been in power since 1933, and young people were more or less automatically enrolled in the Hitler Youth. I had been a Catholic Boy Scout since 1932 in the small town where we lived. At that time, many young boys were Boy Scouts and there was no Hitler Youth; eventually, a few scout masters became Hitler Youth leaders. Such changes were barely perceptible: We traded our green shirts and green ties for brown shirts and ties and kept the same black shorts. We still went hiking and camping and there were no big differences.

There was no active Nazi party in this small town for some time but, later on, a bankrupt little electric shop owner with no standing in town was the boss of the Nazi party. People remembered him as an unsuccessful little merchant, not a very impressive figure. Basically, it was scouting and the things you do as a Boy Scout. That changed when we moved to Marienburg, when I was sixteen.

The national-socialistic indoctrination in the Hitler Youth was continuously conducted by "educators" for the party. We, of course, were very much aware of this process but there was no alternative. It was a very, very slow process, truly imperceptible to those of us young people who were politically inexperienced.

My father was Deutsche National. That would probably be called a right-wing Republican today—very nationalistic—very straight and uncompromising. Three *Deutschnationale Volkspartei (DNVP)* representatives were in Hitler's first cabinet and in three months they were out.

The party leaders at that time were Hugenberg and Düsenberg, from the *Stahlhelm*, the organization of the front-line soldiers of WWI. They were at the very right, but they marched around in uniforms so they were a kind of competition to the *Sturmabteilung* (Storm Troopers, SA) of the Nazi party. On the left, the communists were as organized as the Nazis, and they and the social democrats had their marching *Reichsbanner*, too. They marched on the left, and they also had a uniform of sorts, a cap, and a flag.

THE FLEDGLING TAKES WING

DR. FOX (*continued*). There were about fifteen students during the last two years of my high school in Marienburg. We were sick and tired of marching around and singing Hitler Youth songs. So, the entire class decided to enroll in the glider-flying Hitler Youth.

I was not overly mechanically or mathematically inclined, but before my glider involvement I was in the Motor Hitler Youth. My education was comprehensive and some mechanical things were taught, but I was never gifted that way. We had a little 125 DKW motorcycle which we took apart and put together, so I would say my knowledge of mechanical things was adequate. Some things were, of course, silly. We didn't have to wear the brown uniforms, but we wore blue uniforms, which were much more attractive to the girls.

Marienburg had a long tradition of glider flying. The world sailplane record-holder, Ferdinand Schultz, was a Marienburg public school teacher. He flew his record flights up on the Kurische Nehring on the Baltic Sea. I think one of these flights lasted thirty-nine hours. Some older guys organized a camp outside town where we young guys learned to fly.

FRAZER. What did you call the sailplane program and what prompted you to join it?

DR. FOX. It was called *segelfliegen* (gliding). One of the reasons for joining was because we wanted to get away from the singing, exercising, and never-ending drills. Most of us had five years of it and we were sick and tired of it; we were looking for something else. My first diversion was the Motor Hitler Youth, just to get away from the other. So I would say I was interested in getting into the *segelfliegen*, but I had no earlier involvement in flying. But then as soon as we got into it, we liked it. And it was, of course, a sport.

The glider was powerless, so friends pulled rubber cords on the sides to launch it. There was no instructor in the glider. You sat ahead of the wing on a seat that was totally in front of the rest of the fuselage. You held what we used to call a "broom stick," and your feet operated the pedals. You ran down the hill forty times a day and pulled the darn thing up again—it was quite heavy—and each of us flew only two or three times a day.

I was just sixteen and I had respect for all that was going on. Our first flight was ten to fifteen yards. You kept increasing the length of the jumps to 200 or 300 yards or so downhill. And when you had five one-minute flights, you got your first Wave recognition insignia—a white dove on a blue background. And as time went on, you got two, three, insignias and people could see how far you had progressed.

Rubberband-powered glider

FRAZER. How many of these short duration flights were required to achieve the third Wave insignia?

DR. FOX. Oh, that took a year and a half—only in the summer season.

FRAZER. Was there a ground school?

DR. FOX. Yes, a lot of it. And then building the darn things; you couldn't buy them. In winters you spent hours and hours every week—two or three afternoons for three or four hours cutting the plywood and gluing it together.

FRAZER. Did you or any of your associates ever have an accident?

DR. FOX. No, nothing serious. The terrain was south of Danzig on the high bank of the Nogat River, which was the easternmost branch of the Vistula (Weichsel) River which goes into the Baltic Sea. That's where we jumped.

FRAZER. How high was that?

DR. FOX. The hill was about fifty to seventy yards high, but we were seldom more than a few feet above the ground. The distance we traveled depended on our skill and if the prevailing wind was strong enough, we could go a greater distance.

This was the summer of 1938 and the war started in 1939. We all had to go to work or into the service. And the war was very close. They bombed the big bridges over the Vistula River thirty kilometers to the west. Many people were drafted, many of our teachers.

WEHRMACHT OR LUFTWAFFE?

FRAZER. Then what happened to you and your siblings?

DR. FOX. I was in my last year in school and, in November 1939, I took the final examination called the Abitur (school-leaving examination) so I could get into university, and I was still seventeen.

The Polish war was over at that point. So everybody my age faced the inevitable question: "When am I going to be drafted?" I probably would have had a little time because I was only seventeen—I became eighteen in February 1940. But I looked around me and explored what happened to other people and a few of my friends from the glider-flying group decided to volunteer for the Air Force. We found out that was probably the smarter way of doing it instead of being drafted into the Army. We had had an Air Force since 1936, and I volunteered for it. This took a little while, but they inducted me on January 15, 1940.

My brother wasn't taken into the Army until three years later. He was to have gone through the *Reichsarbeitsdienst*, the working service which was required before you went into the Army. They dug ditches and did other things and they had uniforms. It was originally for one year and later was shortened to half a year. By 1939, when the war started, it was entirely suspended and we were immediately taken into the Army or the Air Force.

We knew that to become a pilot, you first had to have your Abitur and you had an advantage if you were a glider flyer. So on January 15, 1940, I was taken into the Naval Air Force which was later absorbed into the regular air force. The training for the Naval Air Force was in Schleswig-Holstein, a little province south of Denmark that sticks out of the north of Germany, quite near Hamburg by the North Sea. The training was done, however, on the Baltic Sea. The name of the facility was *Heiligenhafen*, and there I was given a very peculiar education, a complete seaman's training.

I could sail, row, and make knots and I learned all the Morse Code signals—all the international flags—everything connected to seamanship. It was very vigorous training, it was winter and we had to row in the Baltic Sea in February and we thought our hands would freeze off. This lasted exactly six months.

FRAZER. Was your status akin to a midshipman?

DR. FOX. No, I was absolutely the lowest rank, just a soldier. But, during this time, our superiors considered our skills. Those of us who had passed our Abitur could apply for flight training. Then we had to go through a fairly rigorous physical exam. I still remember the doctor was a very nice, captain-ranked, physician and I was a little tense—I was lying on the examining table and he tried to check my reflexes but I was kind of stiff, so he asked if I could name a drama by Shakespeare, and that relaxed me.

BEGINNING IN THE LUFTWAFFE

FRAZER. I learned to fly seaplanes when I was fifteen. This was followed by five flight schools. So I am very interested in your flight training experience. What was involved?

DR. FOX. I passed all the requirements and, on July 1, 1940, was sent to the *Flugzengfürhrerschule* in Warnemunde, near Rostok. Warnemunde is a very nice spa on the Baltic Sea. The school was run by a group of former Lufthansa captains who flew the first flying boats to South America. The most famous one was Wolfgang von Gronau, who flew with Do 18F flying boats. These men seemed old to us, but they were the teachers. Before that, they were famous transoceanic pilots and then they had to teach us!

The day you start in flying school is your "birthday," so to speak, as a pilot—I was 7/40. I got my first pilots license, which was just for small planes, but it was the first license I got, in November 1940, so I was still eighteen.

FRAZER. What kind of planes did you fly?

DR. FOX. We flew a lot of small planes, but also the early fighter planes. These were bi-wing, with open cockpits. There were probably twenty-five different types. We had excellent training which turned out to be very advantageous.

FRAZER. What was the ratio of ground school to flying?

DR. FOX. We had school when the weather was bad, more in fall and winter, less in summer. Often we had more school hours than flying hours.

FRAZER. Was the instruction more or less left to the discretion of your greatly experienced instructors or was it highly regimented?

DR. FOX. The instructors decided everything. The atmosphere in pilot school was much more flyer than soldier. The instructors were very human. They tried hard. If somebody didn't do so well, they gave them more chances— very few flunked out.

FRAZER. How large was your class and how many did you graduate?

DR. FOX. Thirty-five to forty, and about five dropped out. There were two phases of training, A and B. A was in very little planes, and B in fighters. Remember that German aircraft were developed in a very short time—from nothing in 1935 to Stukas in 1939 or 1940.

There wasn't enough time for thorough testing, so all these planes had their peculiarities, and you had to learn all of them. This helped me. The experience that came from coping with these peculiarities, coupled with the good schooling I had, eventually helped me to survive. And the longer the war went on, the shorter and poorer the training. Things had to move quickly; students didn't fly as many different types of aircraft; they didn't get as much flying time; and, in general, their training was not as good.

FRAZER. Okay, but, specifically, what made your training so good?

DR. FOX. The sheer number of different types of aircraft I flew under the close supervision of excellent instructors. Also, the amount of flying time.

FRAZER. Did you fly aerobatics?

DR. FOX. Yes, we had to fly the complete *Kunstflug* program [artistic flight program]. Two or three teachers watched us from the ground and, if you didn't do it right you had to repeat it. The aerobatic plane we flew was the Buecker Jungmeister. This was a bi-plane with a very short wing span.

FRAZER. How do you spell this program? I'm not able to understand what you said.

DR. FOX. Oh, I'm sorry. I should have told you about my accent. After puberty, one's vocal apparatus changes. The muscles and the cartilage involved in the larynx change and that is why people who learn languages later will always have an accent. There is hardly a way around it. Dr. Henry Kissinger came to America when he was fourteen, and his accent is almost worse than mine. Even actors who take advanced training never rid themselves of accents when speaking languages learned as adults. Anyway, the word is K-u-n-s-t-f-l-u-g.

CHOICE TO EXCEL

FRAZER. What followed this rather basic flight training?

DR. FOX. At the end of A and B school, we had to decide what we wanted to do: Become a fighter and keep flying one-engine planes or go on to fly larger planes. The instructors advised us and may have influenced the outcome, but it was basically our decision.

FRAZER. Most U.S. Air Corps bombardiers or navigators in WWII started out in pilot training. Hence this question: Did some of your fellow flight school students become bombardiers or navigators?

DR. FOX. No, all of them were pilots. Many of the navigators and bombardiers had been turned down for pilot training. They were, however, also expected to have passed the Abitur because of the complexity of their assignments. The radio operators typically had less education. The bombardier in a Junkers had little to do because it was a dive bomber; pilots aimed and dropped the bombs. Bombardiers were more or less passengers.

The Heinkel III, which came a little earlier, was larger and had a bombsight. The bombardier advised the pilot about heading-changes on the bomb run. Gunners who also took pictures in the Junkers, pilots, navigators, and radio operators all wore distinctive metal wings on the left side of their chests.

FRAZER. What did you do after the A and B training?

DR. FOX. Even from the beginning of my flight training, I wanted to know more about flying—instruments and night flying, for example. So, I applied for C school. This was multi-engine flying. I started flying the Junkers 86 and the Heinkel III as well as a good number of older biplanes. We started right in with instrument and night flying as well as long-distance flying.

FRAZER. Please tell me any anecdotes or funny stories you remember as we go along.

DR. FOX. At that time, we had very few accidents. In my A and B training, we didn't have any fatalities at all. Oh, occasionally somebody wrecked a plane landing, but mostly harmless things.

One interesting thing happened when I was in C school; I remember we flew a training flight from Berlin to Amsterdam where we had a three-day break. We went to town and had a good time. When we came back to Schiphol airport (the same airport KLM flies into today), we got into our old Junkers 52 again with our instructors and five students. Before we could start, a big truck arrived and loaded our big airplane with large, very peculiar looking boxes. I know now, and probably knew at the time, these probably contained big pictures—paintings.

So, we flew back to Staaken airport in Berlin and the big boxes were taken off. I'm absolutely sure today these were Dutch paintings for Herman Goering. That was 1941. After that, at the end of 1941, in C school, they again divided the student pilots into two groups. The ones who hadn't done too well became transport pilots and the rest of us went on to instrument and night flying school. That was an eight-week course in East Prussia in the small village of Serappen. It was out in the middle of nowhere and it was cold—especially because the Junkers 52 was not heated!

FRAZER. What did you have in the way of flying clothing?

DR. FOX. We were very pampered. What the outside world saw was our beautiful, zippered, suede, fur-lined, knee-high boots. They were very attractive to girls. And we had well-insulated flying outfits.

We lived simply, but the schooling was very intensive, especially when we moved into C group for night and instrument flying. We had to learn celestial navigation, which was quite stressful for me because I wasn't mathematically inclined. But overall, the training was excellent.

After this training, we received our instrument ratings, which meant we could fly any type or size of plane with any number of engines day or night and in any kind of weather. This all took two years, I was well-trained and my rating was the highest obtainable.

CHOOSING HOW TO FIGHT

DR. FOX (continued). There weren't too many choices for men who were trained in this way; we were to fly bombers. So I was sent to bomber school in Hersching, near Linz, in Austria. At this point, we flew the bombers we would have to fly in combat. The options included the Dornier Do 17, or Do 217, "the flying pencil," with the two-rudder tail, the Junkers 88, and the Heinkel III. I didn't like the slow and clumsy Heinkel III. You could see it was outdated, and I'm glad I wasn't posted to one of those outfits. In the spring and summer of 1942, although Norway and the Balkans had fallen and we were far into Russia, things there didn't look so good.

We knew what was going on; the pilots we came into contact with at different airports talked, and it was evident the air war in Germany had turned. More German cities were being bombed than we were bombing outside Germany.

In any case, we practiced with wooden bombs and were tested and graded. There, for the first time, we were also given our crew. We were supposed to be able to pick our crews, but as a practical matter, officers would say "you fly with him" or "you fly with them." So, I got my crew. Interestingly, all four of us wound up with graduate degrees after the war!

FRAZER. Were you an aircraft commander?

DR. FOX. Well, there was only one pilot. Only the big Condor 200 and maybe some seaplanes had co-pilots but they were so rare you didn't see many of them.

AUTHOR'S NOTE. Allied bomber missions flown in WWII had a seldom-considered advantage over those flown by the Luftwaffe; they all had co-pilots. After-mission reports and personal narratives of Allied bomber crews again and again pointed up why this was so important. Many American bombing missions were flown deep into Germany and savaged by Luftwaffe fighters and shells from antiaircraft guns (flak). Many aircraft commanders (A/Cs) were killed or so seriously wounded that co-pilots had to take over and fly badly damaged airplanes back to their bases. Co-pilots had exactly the same training as pilots in command. Escaping by parachute, however, was the only alternative for Luftwaffe crewmembers if their pilot was killed or too badly wounded to fly.

CHOICES—ALL OF THEM BAD

FRAZER. With this progression of training, you were obviously getting closer to the point when you would have to fly combat. How were you feeling about that?

DR. FOX. It's hard to say. We knew very well losses in the air war were very high—far above fifty percent. We had lost many friends and acquaintances. Some of the men I trained with in A and B school who went on to fly fighters were shot down while I was in C school, and we read about them in the newspapers. One of my original group, 7/40, was already famous. But we knew the losses were tremendous. This was after we lost the air war over England and we knew that this was certainly a defeat for the entire German Air Force.

Goring had promised Hitler that we would win the war from the air but we lost, and lost and lost. By the time the Russian front opened in 1941, we were spread very thin. Just looking at the current map, you could see that everything forecast to be captured and occupied remained uncaptured and unoccupied. It was obvious that we had fallen far short of our goals. Any reasonably intelligent person had to know the inevitable outcome. Certainly, the chance of surviving a lengthy war was not very good. We were not overly scared; we were probably fatalistic. There was no way out—of not doing it or getting out.

The critical point for us Germans was the moment the war with Russia started. We knew if we didn't win in Russia, we were doomed. And that kept many, many people going. Just think of the US and the Cold War. What kept the Germans spending billions and billions? Fear of the Russians. It simply was out of the question for an individual to give up. If you tried to quit, they'd shoot you or put you someplace where you would go under anyway. I'm not sure Americans can really understand how it felt to have your back against the wall this way.

"Know all and you will pardon all."

THOMAS A'KEMPIS

A FRIEND IN NEED—FIRST
COMBAT ASSIGNMENT

FRAZER. What happened after you finished the bomber school and were assigned a crew?

DR. FOX. Before I tell you what happened next, I should mention that I was not an officer except by default at the end of the war. I had been enrolled as a medical student in Danzig, so I was not on the officer's career track.

For some reason, in Austria I was taken by railroad to Barth, close to the Baltic Sea, to an airport where there were about 150 crewmembers. We were told we would be divided up for posting to different bombing groups stationed at various fronts. So we were all lined up in good Prussian order, with the pilot in front of the crew.

A captain matter of factly read off our assignments. Our crew was assigned to *Kampfgeschwader* (bomber group) KG2, an outfit that flew the Dornier 217, which had a high wing and big engines. They flew against England and had terrible

Kurt Fox's Ju 88, in which he flew mostly night missions

losses—maybe the highest of all. This would have required me to move from the Junkers 88s to 217s and I'd never flown a 217.

I was standing there more or less resigned to my fate. Then, among the group of officers gathered in front of us, I saw a face I remembered; it was my best friend from glider-flying days. He and I went to dance school together in our last year of high school and played tennis all the time. We had been best of friends, but now he was a lieutenant. Nevertheless, I broke all the tenets of discipline and called "Harold!" I was a mere sergeant at that time and just shouldn't have called him by his first name in front of the others. But he was overjoyed at seeing me and quickly asked where I had been assigned. I told him KG2 and he said, "Oh, you come with me to the KG54 in Sicily." So, he went to the captain and had him change my assignment—and probably saved my life.

So we went to Italy. KG54 was an old outfit because it had the skull and bones, which had to do with the black hussars under Frederick the Great. It was a cavalry unit with bear-skin black helmets with the cross bones on the sides. I had heard about this outfit and remembered that they fought in the Mediterranean and, briefly, in Russia.

My friend and I were in the same bomber group almost to the end, and he is still living although not very well—he was almost blind when I visited him last March. He never flew as much as I did. He became the aide to Commander Colonel Freiherr Riedesel zu Eisenbach of the bomber group, who was eventually killed in an ME 262 in Munich eight days before the war ended. General Adolf Galland was in the same group and survived. Colonel Steinhoff was also in this group and, despite disfiguring burns to his face, became commander of the German Air Force after the war.

We were held back from the front for a while when we arrived in Sicily. Each bomber group had four smaller groups which were supposed to have had forty-five crewmembers each. All through the war, to the last day, I don't think we ever had more than ten or twelve crewmembers, and usually only four or five. Anyway, the fourth group was always the training group, and it trained crews for the particular missions they would have to fly. In the Mediterranean, our principal mission was to sink ships.

AUTHOR'S NOTE. Dr. Fox was extremely forthright when we interviewed him, and it was apparent he had an encyclopedic memory. Yet, at no point did he mention that he or his fellow Luftwaffe associates were underfed. In fact, he made a point of telling us that Luftwaffe personnel were very well cared for in every way. But the men in the following two pictures (p. 50) look malnourished, at least regarding their very thin arms and legs. Dr. Fox did mention that he was

Fox crew between flights on Boot of Italy

Fox Crew on pile of old stone ruins in Olive Grove, where they lived while in Grottaglie, Italy

a Prisoner of War from May 8 through December 1945, in a Camp for German Officers at Attichy, France, and when discharged, he weighed only ninety ponds, whereas his "normal weight" (perhaps later in life), was 160. Neither his son, Chris, nor any of his close friends we have asked about this, have shed any light on this apparent discrepancy.

IMPOTENT ALLY,
WANING EFFECTIVENESS

DR. FOX (*continued*). The convoys the British sent from Gibraltar to Alexandria to Cairo should have been attacked by the Italian Navy but our dear associates, the Italians, didn't do anything—the huge, very impressive Italian Navy was lying in Taranto and we were in Grottaglie.

Our fourth group, the training group, was about fifty miles from Taranto in the boot of Italy. We trained for bombing ships by dropping cement bombs on floating practice targets. These practice bombs at 500 kilograms were quite similar to the real thing we'd be using later. We did this for about eight weeks. Then, suddenly, my crew was moved to the 3rd Group in Catania, Sicily, right below Mt. Aetna, which was very nice because you could always see it smoking, or glowing, or spitting day or night.

At the same time it was kind of depressing because we went into St. Georges Hotel in Catania [it's still there and I've been there once since the war] and each *staffel*, which

Kurt Fox (third from left)

was supposedly the smallest unit—twelve to fifteen crew-members—had one floor in the hotel. We walked around and there was nobody there. Our crew had only five and this was not encouraging.

After this, I acquired a new navigator because my original navigator couldn't tolerate diving attacks; every time we dove in training, he started crying! I didn't think that was a good prospect for the future, so I went to my boss, the captain, and said, "Look, I can't put up with this." And he said, "Well, I'll see." That evening a master sergeant came to my room and I knew he was the navigator for the captain of the group. His name was Master Sergeant Rudi Maurer, and his decorations showed he had flown at least 100 missions, and I had none. He said, "I hear you need a navigator, would you take me?" He was three years older and, by rank, much higher. I was flabbergasted, but readily agreed.

FRAZER. Why do you think he wanted to do this?

Sight-seeing at St. George's Hotel, Catania, Italy

DR. FOX. His pilot lost his nerve. He developed a fear of landing and turned back from missions before completing them, so his navigator was quite right in seeking a new pilot. But I was the youngest pilot in the group. Why he chose me I'll never know. Perhaps it was some kind of instinct.

I was a bit intimidated by his age, rank, and, most of all, his experience, but we got along very well, especially after the playing field levelled a bit. I'll never forget how it happened. It was October 22, 1942, the night Rommel turned around at El Alamein. We flew from Catania to bomb the front lines. Soon after take-off, we dropped down to 150 feet over the Mediterranean so the radar in Malta wouldn't pick us up. I felt we might be a bit off course and I asked Sergeant Maurer if we weren't a bit too far left. He didn't answer right away; the maps were in sections, and I assumed

Kurt Fox (second from left) with Ju 88 Crew

he was taking time to unfold them. He finally sheepishly admitted that he had forgotten the map!

There we were flying over the Mediterranean at 1:00 A.M. flying to an airport I had never seen in Crete with 2,000 kilos in bombs and no map. So I asked the sergeant, "Have you ever been to Crete?" "Oh," he said, "many times, I know how it looks." I asked if he could see it at night and he said yes that we could. I said, "All right, we'll hold a little more to the right to the west side of Crete, fly along the coast, and then we'll run into Iraclion." We did so. Afterward he jumped out of the plane when we landed and ran to the command post to get a new map!

THE BEGINNING OF THE END

So, we departed Crete and bombed El Alamein. Rommel never got that far again; the war had changed. The same week Stalingrad went sour. I was in at the bad end of this bad war.

Rommel had to kill himself on July 20, 1944, because of his part in the plot to kill Hitler. I remember that date well. We were in Eindhoven, Holland, and I had flown fifty missions in the west, bombing the advancing Allies' ports and airfields.

Someone came running down the steps of the high school where we were billeted and yelled that an attempt had been made on Hitler's life, but he had survived. I've always wondered what the fighting Air Force would have done if he had been killed.

Would they have trusted the Army officers, the nobility, who were involved in the plot? I'm not sure. That would have been a big "if." The question could never be answered because we lost the war unconditionally. There was never again the possibility of reviving these ideas that came out of World War I, some of which led to Hitler's power.

We tied two German soldiers to hardware inside the bomb bay so we could bring them back to Sicily with us. But 150,000 were captured, many of whom were interned in America. There were 3,000 at Ft. Crawford, Nebraska, and they were very popular, some married American girls, and every two years these Germans captured in Africa still meet there.

FRAZER. Where were you flying from at this juncture?

DR. FOX. Catania, from which my unit flew most of its missions to Malta, only thirty minutes away, and that's where we suffered the greatest losses. My new navigator had already flown twenty-five missions against Malta, so that helped me very much. We flew with two or three other planes a night to bomb Malta.

AUTHOR'S NOTE. The Junkers Ju 88 was a German World War II twin-engine, multi-role combat aircraft. Designed in the mid-1930s as a "fast bomber." It became one of the most versatile combat aircraft of the war. More than 16,000 Ju 88s were built with dozens of variants flown on a wide variety of missions. Interestingly, when armed with rockets, it brought down a number of Allied B-17s by trailing their formations and firing from the rear.

Dr. Fox flew most of his missions as a dive-bomber. The angle of the dive was about forty-five degrees. His airspeed in these dives was about 450 miles per hour. His Ju 88 had dive brakes but he seldom used them. When he pulled out,

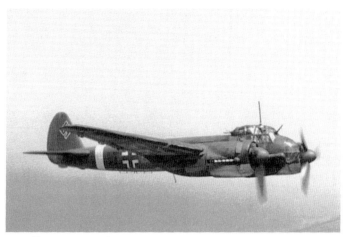

Ju 88 (from Wikipedia)

the force of gravity was typically between 2.5 and 4, always causing the pilot to black out.

Interestingly, the Junkers had an automatic pull-out device; after the bombs were released, it took over and pulled the plane out of the dive just as the pilot was blacking out. It was as though a curtain came down and then you'd wake up just as the horizon appeared in a shallow climb. You'd get used to this, and it never bothered the crew much.

DR. FOX (continued). The Allies had submarines in rock tunnels so we couldn't get at them, so we kept hitting the town and the airport. They had a tremendous defense with anti-aircraft fire and, worse, night fighters. They were the best night fighters; they had come down from England—P-38 Lightnings for the most part—and they were good and very nasty.

I flew only about four or five attacks on Malta. We were moved because, pretty soon, the invasion of Africa by the

Allies began. These were the last days of October 1942. It was amazing I survived; every time I flew with other aircraft, some of them didn't come back. If I flew with four, two didn't come back and when I flew with three, one didn't come back—we never came back with a full complement. These odds were always in the forefront of our thinking.

My experienced navigator helped me a lot. He knew the night fighter tactics, what to watch for and what to do when they came. We always maintained radio silence; we never talked with the ground or each other, but the Allies did. We knew the frequencies they used and we'd listen to their chatter; when the volume became louder, we knew they were very close. They used first names and I remember one was Peter; I heard him talk again later when I flew over London. I'm sure it was the same guy. The number of pilots who did these special things was very small on our side and the other. The Allies had about thirty night fighter pilots—not many more—but they were very, very good and highly experienced.

"Before we can forgive one another, we
have to understand one another."

═══════════════════════

EMMA GOLDMAN

ONE AGAINST MANY

DR. FOX (*continued*). We started on the other side of Africa; we knew they were coming down from England. On the morning of November 9, 1942, we started from Catania and flew reconnaissance missions in prescribed corridors generally west and about fifteen miles wide. We flew as far west as our fuel permitted—600 or 800 miles—and doubled back east in the adjacent corridor.

Heading east in our second assigned corridor, we flew along the African coast. The weather was beautiful and clear, and about noon, on the other side of Algiers, we came upon a sight which I will not forget as long as I live: 700 ships! There were three aircraft carriers, five battleships and everything else: 700 ships in the Bay of Algiers.

My gunner had a robot camera that would automatically advance frames and he started taking pictures of the ships. We had only one 250-kilo bomb because we left our usual bomb load behind to make room for extra gas to give us more range for reconnaissance. Well, good German soldiers didn't waste bombs; they have to drop them on somebody. So, from 12,000 feet the best target looked like an aircraft carrier. There was a lot of well-aimed fire coming up from the ships and, just a couple of seconds into our diving bomb run, we took a hit on the bottom of the plane. My gunner's elbow was blown away and the hit got me into a bad position. In correcting it, I had to maneuver violently and this threw off the trajectory of the bomb. Eventually, it hit right alongside the carrier.

Our airplane was damaged; I didn't know how badly, but at least it still handled well. Thank God, I had an idea. It didn't seem likely the ship gunners could depress their weapons and shoot down. So I dove to within a few feet of the water, well below the decks of the larger ships, and I vividly remember the crewmembers looking down at us with their mouths open! We had enough speed to get out of the range of the ships and head northeast toward Sardinia.

We were just out of the harbor when the right engine coughed and stopped running. I was able to feather the right propeller so we could just barely maintain low-level altitude, twenty feet or so over the water. Things seemed to be turning out pretty well.

But our smiles disappeared when we noticed three Spitfires were after us. They started an interesting routine: They flew toward our rear in trail. The first one fired at us full blast and, just before he rammed us, he turned left and rejoined the trail formation at the rear as the second moved in for the kill. The third followed, repeating the procedure, and they kept this up for what seemed an eternity. I made all the evasive maneuvers I dared with one engine out, but my options were limited.

This was my first daytime mission and thus the first time I had actually seen enemy aircraft attacking me. The rear-facing twin machine guns were knocked out and I still have a souvenir piece of glass from my fortified window. Finally, the apparent leader of the fighter formation pulled up very close to my left wing and half-waved, half-saluted as if to say "We're out of ammunition, but there will be another day!"

DR. FOX'S SON, CHRIS, REMEMBERS HEARING HIS FATHER TALK ABOUT THIS ENCOUNTER. Dad was overwhelmed with this guy's fairness. Dad always felt the need for fairness—it ran very deep with him.

DR. FOX. The one remaining engine continued running quite smoothly and, without any bombs and having used up most of our fuel, I was actually able to regain a little altitude—up to about 2,500 feet. And I knew about the Elmas airport, which is on the southern coast of Sardinia on a flat river delta without obstructions.

I had made three successful wheels-up landings in the past without serious damage. In retrospect, though, I realize I did one thing I might not have done later in my career. When the landing gear would not extend hydraulically, I pumped it down manually. But the flaps wouldn't budge, so we knew we'd have to land at an unusually high airspeed. The tires had been shot through as well, because, when we touched down, the rubber peeled off the wheels and we skidded along on the rims.

When we finally stopped, one of my crew realized that he would have to pull our badly wounded gunner though the exit hatch which had a ladder that you usually extended. He jumped down and blood cascaded down the ladder before

Fox Ju 88 after being shot down in 1942. Airplane was riddled with 88 holes from the attacking English Spitfires.

he could help his wounded comrade. There were eighty-eight holes in the airplane, and a journalist who covered our theater was right on the spot taking pictures which appeared, along with a widespread story.

The gunner survived but had a stiff arm from then on and never flew again. The airplane was scrapped.

We had two days' rest before we were flown back to our base and resumed combat missions. Our beleaguered forces held onto Tunisia for quite a while, so we bombed the well-defended harbors along the North African coast.

A SINKING TO REMEMBER

DR. FOX (*continued*). It was obvious the next landing would be in Sicily. On July 10, 1943, the Allies landed in Gela, Sicily, on the middle of the southern coast. We were tasked with bombing one of the convoys heading for the landing, and we had to arrange to arrive at first morning's light. It was still dark as we approached the target zone from the east, but suddenly we saw the phosphorescence wake from a very fast-moving ship. The wake looked as bright as a neon light.

It was almost certainly a destroyer, which meant it was narrow and hard to hit. I decided on a gliding attack rather than our usual forty-degree dive. As we closed in, the ship fired at us with its fairly light armament, but none of its fire came close. So we dropped four 500-kilogram bombs. We were going quite fast and, as we pulled up and away from the ship, the radio operator looked back and said, "Oh, we got a hit." We recorded a hit on an enemy war-ship, realizing it couldn't have been a freighter.

USS Maddox, DD-622, launched just six months before its sinking

As it turned out, it was the destroyer USS Maddox (DD-622) [not DD-731, famous for its role in the Bay of Tonkin]. According to men from the ship I would later meet, it was a brand new ship—less than six months old—and this was its first mission in the Mediterranean.

I later learned that there were 210 crewmembers below decks and seventy-four on deck when one or two of our bombs hit depth charges stored on the fantail. Those on deck jumped or were blown into the water and were picked up, but those below went down with the ship in just ninety seconds. It was said to have been the fastest sinking of a ship in WWII!

There was no immediate assessment of this heart-rending damage by either side. Nevertheless, I knew in my heart that it had to have been a severe loss and this haunted me for much of my life. Eventually, three decades later, a totally unexpected invitation enabled me to meet most of the Maddox survivors. For me and for them, finally meeting face-to-face was a truly liberating experience.

AUTHOR'S NOTE. Every time I delve into research or conduct another interview about the sinking of the USS Maddox (DD-622), I unearth something new and interesting. Dr. Fox, for example, says it was the "phosphorescent" wake that called his attention to the Maddox. Scientists now call this phenomenon "bioluminescence," and it is caused when dinoflagellates, microorganisms in algae, are agitated—as happens when ships exceed certain speeds. Well, all 3,200 Allied ships in the Sicily invasion armada that included the USS Maddox were ordered to hold their speed to eight knots. The skipper of the Maddox realized he was way out of his assigned position and increased the ship's speed to twenty-five knots to get back to where he should have been.

The "talker," Joe Sullivan, whose job it was to relay commands from the captain to the engine room, was on the bridge with a couple of other crewmen and they all asked the Captain to reconsider. He nevertheless ordered "full speed ahead." These recollections were nearly unanimous at Maddox survivor meetings.

The sinking of the USS Maddox cut short many promising careers; few more so than that of Ensign Robert Crathorne. At thirty-four, he was one of the older crewmembers, and he didn't have to serve. He was married, and a well-established and highly respected attorney with a top flight organization, National Life Insurance Company in Vermont, now National Life Group.

Ensign A. Robert Crathorne. Courtesy National Life Group

He consulted with his boss, Deane C. Davis (future governor of Vermont) about leaving the company to serve during WWII. Davis encouraged him to serve, probably with a promise to hold a position until after the war.

"As you envision God's forgiveness of you,
you will be able to forgive others."

CHUCK SWINDOLL

INEVITABLE DEFEAT,
LAST DITCH EFFORTS

FRAZER. As you and your crew confronted inevitable defeat did you become less diligent in performing your duties? Did your commanders?

DR. FOX. If we, as a crew, became less diligent it was an unconscious thing. We continued to put our lives on the line against an ever more dangerous enemy. With the exception of the brave men who attempted to kill Hitler, I think this was largely true of our commanders. However, this was difficult to determine because there was such a gap between our ranks.

Still in all, there was a near universal perception that all of Germany, with few exceptions, felt we had been cheated—treated unjustly—at the end of WWI. Setting that right seemed to be part of Hitler's policy. The first thing was of course the war against Poland to get rid of the Polish Corridor that cut East Prussia off. That's how it started. Well, it started earlier; it started with the reoccupation of the Rhineland in 1936, which was supposed to have been demilitarized. Then, of course, the Sudetenland thing and Czechoslovakia. But I came in at the beginning of the downhill slide, because Africa was finally lost.

Commanders or, better, scientists, came up with interesting new weapons at this point. For example, we dropped a torpedo with a parachute. When it hit the water, it was programmed to run on a triangular course to hit ships inside the harbors. This was the winter of 1942 and 1943.

When the Allies landed on southern Sicily, we had to move. You can't stay very close to the front lines with a big bomber, so we went back to Grottaglie, on the boot of Italy. From there we bombed Sicily, especially Syracuse Harbor, south of Catania, where we hit two large freighters.

Once again we had to move, this time to Foggia, a large flat area on the Adriatic coast. We had six airfields in the area and they were all so primitive our gas was delivered by trucks. There were no enemy attacks and our missions were to fly as needed in the Mediterranean area.

The next invasion was Anzio, south of Naples. It was number three for me. From there the Allies—Americans, really—moved to Monte Cassino. This was a month-long, very bloody confrontation. The Germans defended high ground and natural defenses, so it took a particularly high toll of American troops.

We had to leave that part of Italy for Bergamo, just north of Milan at the foot of the Alps. This was November 1943. It was a terrible place to fly, just like the Rocky Mountains with awful weather. I flew the first night and several subsequent missions against the Allies when they invaded Corsica. We, and other *staffels*, were almost completely out of crewmembers. We desperately needed replacements but

Camouflaged aircraft (note plant material on propellers)

were nevertheless moved over the Alps to Ingolstadt in southern Germany about 100 miles northeast of Munich.

CHRIS FOX. Dad went to Munich for two weeks' leave. This was because he had trained in Bavaria and had left a couple of personal things with a farm family near Munich because he traveled light when he was in combat. Just before D-Day, Dad was on a train evacuating Munich during an Allied bombing attack. This was where he met my Mother and her mom, who said, "I know someone in the Luftwaffe. His name is Otto Blersch." And my dad said, "I know Otto Blersch," and he pulled from his wallet a pass-like thing

Lieutenant Kurt Fox about the time he met his future wife Trudy

that showed that Blersch was his senior officer and had just assigned him his gas mask.

It was sort of love at first sight with my mom, but Dad was called back to fly on D-Day. Otto Blersch was also there flying out of Marx—only a very small number of airplanes flew on D-Day—I think it was 35 bombers and 110 fighters.

ENGLAND AGAIN

DR. FOX *(continued)*. We hadn't flown against England for quite a while, not since 1940 or 1941. Our goal was to equalize the Allies' considerable air power advantage and disturb the invasion preparations.

FRAZER. Was the period between the time you first started flying combat in October 1942 and the end of the war less or more dangerous than from the beginning of the war to when you started?

DR. FOX. As far as flying over England was concerned, it was much more dangerous later during the war because England's defenses were incomparably better then.

Surprisingly, we got forty-five new crewmembers, which was a lot, and it greatly buoyed our morale. This good news was short-lived however; these people were simply not well trained. This soon became very evident; these inexperienced crews simply disappeared. It was pathetic.

Our tactics changed at this point, especially regarding the way we worked. From the spring of 1944 until the Normandy invasion we set off from Germany and attacked England, but we never returned to our point of departure. We flew back to Marx in northern Germany, Eindhoven in northern Holland, Villacoublay in southern France, and Trondheim, Norway.

We never came back to the same place, but every place we eventually landed we nevertheless had a bed and something to eat. The reason for this was that, with their new radar and sophisticated aerial reconnaissance, the Allies knew our point of departure and started sending night fighters to intercept us when we returned. Landing at other bases thus helped us save some aircraft and crews.

We lost many of our new crewmembers at night, not just from enemy action; many were simply disoriented. It was tragic to see the new crewmembers and predict all too accurately which would make it and which would not. Our commanders understandably tried an experiment to give new pilots an orientation. They would have them ride as navigators with experienced pilots on bombing missions over England.

Over London, whether in a lone aircraft or in formation, 800 searchlights, 15 thousand flak guns, 30 night fighters, and 150 balloons would try to bring us down. If we were caught in a searchlight, we'd have to maneuver violently to escape or a night fighter would be on our tail.

I remember once a night fighter came at us head on, shooting all the time. I had no idea how he'd break off his attack, up, down, to the left, or to the right. Fortunately, I dove down and he pulled up, but this was a rare form of attack. In any case, our first-time pilots, acting as navigators, were petrified. But it wasn't exactly comforting for us veteran pilots; we were used to our regular navigators, and these sightseers were of no help at all.

We were most afraid of the night fighters; the ack-acks didn't seem to bother us that much. This was surprising because we were not that fast—only about 280 kilometers per hour when we were loaded.

FRAZER. You've referred to Junkers (Ju 88s) as a dive bombers. Were they always deployed that way?

DR. FOX. When we first bombed England, in 1940 and 1941, it was blanket, strategic bombing with no need to hit targets precisely, and Junkers-type planes would fly straight and level bomb runs. But as the need to hit tactical targets evolved, we almost always delivered our bombs from a dive. We wanted to avoid ground fire by diving, picking up a lot of speed, and getting out of the way as fast as we could. Then we'd stay as low as possible to stay under the radar.

Our aiming devices were crude and not overly effective. This may sound inappropriate, but it was, in a certain sense, like a sport. Our skills developed with practice. Col. Rudel disabled more than 1,000 Russian tanks with an eight-centimeter gun attached to a Junkers 87. This was a finely honed skill.

NEW CHALLENGE AND A LITTLE HOPE

DR. FOX (*continued*). I had fifty-three missions prior to Normandy, then during and following the invasion I flew another fifty-six missions, and we had a big celebration when I passed the 100 mark. After Normandy, when the Americans had come through Holland and Belgium and were practically at the Rhine, we dropped our bombers at an airfield in Westphalia and were sent by train to Neuburg in southern Germany.

It was there that we were informed we had to become jet pilots! There was a big fight about it; the fighter pilots wanted to fly them because the Me 262 was basically a fighter. But to fly the 262 in Europe in any weather and possibly at night, you had to have pilots who can do that. Some of the young fighter pilots at that time had only ten weeks of flight training! They didn't know where they were; they flew only in formation up and down from one airport. So the decision was to have the bomber pilots fly the jets and it worked very well.

Pilots gathered in front of Me 262 Jet; Kurt Fox back to camera.

Along with two other pilots, I was sent to the Messer-schmitt factory at Leipheim near Augsburg and we were trained in a two-seat version of the Me 262. One fuel tank had been removed and we sat in tandem with the student in front and the instructor in back. We made three touch-and-go landings and that was it. Then I trained our entire group in November 1944. By March 1945, the Americans were already in Frankfurt. We had forty-two Me 262s camouflaged in bunkers fairly close together but, after the Americans came over with 450 bombers, only one ME 262 could be restored.

I was a lieutenant by this time and commanded a group of seven other pilots. We were sent by train to Prague, the only non-destroyed airport in Europe. This was because the Americans stopped at the Bavarian-Czechoslovakian border since they were hoping to bring in the Czech exile government by air from London. We knew, however, that the Russians were coming in from the other side and they would occupy the entire country. There were forty or fifty Me 262s—it was like a used-car lot. So, we started flying from there and attacked Russian convoys from Breslau to Berlin on the autobahn.

The Me 262s had four 30 mm guns and fourteen rockets. Firing the rockets gave you a peculiar feeling because the plane almost kept up with them for several seconds. But our armaments and tactics were devastating against the Russians.

The Americans, however, kept trying to shoot us down. They orbited over the airport with P-51 Mustangs to prey on us as we slowed for our approach.

LES QUERRY, A CLOSE FRIEND OF DR. FOX, REMEMBERS HEARING HIM RECALL ONE SUCH EVENT. Kurt was strafed by a "red tail" P-51 Mustang flown by a Tuskegee Airman as he landed and before the aircraft stopped rolling. He dove out of the cockpit and into a muddy ditch just before his plane blew up. He found himself next to a major who had had the same experience. Years later when he met the major in a Munich restaurant he asked the major if he recognized him. The major replied that "it was difficult without all of the mud on your face!" Kurt said the major had been a famous glider pilot.

DR. FOX (continued). We developed a very effective countermeasure: we installed anti-aircraft guns a few hundred yards from the ends of the runways and gunners would shoot down our pursuers when they chased us on final approach. Then, on the 4th or 5th of May, we knew the war would be over at 6:00 A.M. on the 8th.

FRAZER. What was the total number of missions you flew?

DR. FOX. More than 100 against the Allies in the west—I don't count the ones I flew against the Russians in the 262. There must have been fifteen or so of those.

I don't think there were many people who flew during four invasions, and one of my last at Normandy was particularly memorable. An order came down to attack from the land at last light—about 8:30 P.M. This was the only time we flew formation in all my flying career. There were colonels following me; it was strange. We came low over the dunes exactly as planned and hit the beaches, which were strewn with all manner of men and equipment, and headed toward ships standing off shore that had already unloaded.

Each of the many ships was protected by a balloon and this was dangerous for us; you couldn't see the cables that might have easily cut off our wings. I remember standing on one wing, sandwiching my way between ships and their balloons. It was a pointless, tragic, mission; we started with fifteen aircraft and only nine returned.

FRAZER. How many pilots had as many missions as you did?

DR. FOX. We didn't count missions as diligently as the Allies. Some fighter pilots had hundreds of kills, but these were against the Russians. Some in our theater had more than 200. Many pilots who flew in the early stages of the war, for example, during the Battle of Britain, were promoted to higher positions and they didn't fly much afterward. Of course, there were a few in the lower ranks who kept on flying, but they were in the minority.

At the end of the war, only about fifteen or twenty percent of pilots who flew during the Battle of Britain were still alive. I was one of the few survivors in my unit; the attrition was terrible. I flew constantly without a break for two and a half years. Ironically, the Air Force had a rest-and-recreation facility and, although all members of my crew had been there earlier, I wasn't scheduled to go there until October 1944. So I did get this little bit of rest just before I started flying jets.

AFTER HOSTILITIES

DR. FOX (*continued*). We certainly didn't want to be taken prisoner by the Russians. So, with my seven pilots, I confiscated a beautiful Steyer six-wheel half-track. We had machine guns, bazookas, pistols, and hand grenades. Discipline had gone by the way and other German soldiers wanted this beautiful vehicle, too. So we headed west and timed it so that we were at the middle of a big American-occupied bridge at 6:00 A.M., at the war's end.

We threw our weapons into the water and the GIs took our wristwatches. At that time there was a stream of German soldiers heading west and the Americans didn't stop anybody, they just let everybody go. We ended up on a little airport I knew at Eger. The Americans had stationed a few tanks around the area and this became our first prison camp.

We were quite peaceful and very glad to be alive. We stayed in this first makeshift camp for about two weeks. They had us type discharge papers for boys fourteen and under and men sixty-five and older. I'm not much of a typist, but I did the best I could. Within a few days, an American captain tapped me on the shoulder and asked if I was Lieutenant Fox. When I said, "Yes," he said, "Follow me." They drove our group captain and me to Plzeň in a jeep. Right in the center of the city was a big hotel I had visited before, the Grand Hotel. As we walked in, I asked my captain what he thought they'd do with us; I said I thought they might send us back to Prague. He said, "Well, maybe."

As we walked into this huge old-fashioned hotel with its marble and antique decor, we saw an assemblage of *Schutzstaffel* (protection squadron or defense corps, SS) generals and senior police of the former occupied Czechoslovakia sitting together in the lobby. I thought, "Oh, oh, this is bad company." But we were taken up to a room where there were two young American guys from West Virginia, and they had a machine gun. It was the middle of the day and they were walking up and down the room with their machine gun. I was afraid they'd shoot us by mistake.

They wouldn't tell us why we were there or what was going to happen but soon took us to another jeep and to the nearby airport. We boarded a C-47 transport plane and sat across from the same two nervous guys with their machine guns as we flew to Frankfurt. Then we were driven to Wiesbaden to a villa, and I looked up and saw somebody sitting on the lawn in a lounging chair reading a newspaper, a civilian elderly guy. It was Gen. Franz Halder, former Chief of the Army General Staff. He was an outspoken critic of several Nazi plans and programs and was relieved of his command and imprisoned in 1942.

We went inside and there was an assemblage of German scientists and military leaders. One of the most interesting men in the group was Professor Esau, who had headed the Kaiser Wilhelm Institute for Chemistry. He said, "Don't worry about the A-bomb, we couldn't do it because when we lost electricity in Norway, we couldn't make heavy water." Then our captors divided us into groups: Navy, Air Force, and civilians and we flew to London.

There we were put into an interrogation camp for German Air Force officers where we met the real Col. King we knew from movies. He was so tall he had to bend down to go through doorways.

We stayed there for about three weeks, where I was interrogated by two American captains. The one who spoke reasonably good German asked me if I would fly the Me 262 for the Americans against the Japanese. This was a big surprise, and I probably hesitated about twenty seconds before saying, "No, I have survived ninety-five crewmembers in my flight unit. I am only twenty-three and I've had enough." Oddly enough, they never asked me again.

My former commanding officer was in the same camp and as we were walking along the perimeter fence he asked, "Fox, did they ask you?" And I said "Yes, and I turned them down." He said, "That's all right, I did, too." America didn't have an operational jet and I now know at least 150 Me 262s were taken to America, so I understand why they wanted to draw on our experience with it. In retrospect, I believe the reason they didn't press to have us fly them was because, with the dropping of the atomic bomb at Hiroshima in August 1945, it became obvious the Japanese surrender was imminent.

From the internment camp in England, we were sent to Sainte-Mère-Église, a little town close to the landing area in Normandy, near the big cemetery you always see in pictures.

I had bombed it four times during the invasion because it was just inland from the first landing sites.

Finally, we went to Attichy, a large American camp for German officers near Compiegne, northeast of Paris. That was a difficult place; we had little tents and beds of straw on top of the dirt with just one army blanket. The food was wretched and the portions ridiculously small. People got sick. People died. I stayed there until December 15, 1945. I weighed 90 pounds when I left and I now weigh 160.

Following our miserable stay in Attichy, we were suddenly shipped to southern Germany in cattle cars and I was discharged on December 17, 1945, at age twenty-three, in Bad Aibling, southeast of Munich.

FREE TO DO WHAT?

DR. FOX (*continued*). Being in prison camp for so long, from May 8, 1945, to December 17, 1945, I had lots of time to think about what I really wanted to do with the rest of my life.

I had no home and no idea where my parents were—nor did they know where I was. The Red Cross card we were allowed to send one day after we were captured arrived at the little farm in Bavaria on December 19, two days after I was discharged.

As it turned out, my parents had escaped at the last minute by ship from Danzig and they were in Güstrow-Mecklenburg, in the eastern sector, north of Berlin. I could not visit East Germany at that time and no former German officer could go to medical school in East Germany.

At ninety pounds, I was too weak for three weeks to do much, and very nice, very poor Bavarian farmers fed me. Pretty soon, I could do manual work as a laborer in the local brewery. I cut ice in the winter, fed the animals, and worked like a demon until March 1946. It was hard to adjust to this new role; one day I had been a glamorized pilot flying Germany's newest and fastest fighters and now I was living the same life as these villagers.

The reason I went to this particular farm was because I had lived with families in the same village when I was flying the Me 262. The field had been bombed constantly and there was no living there at night, so, the barracks at the field were used only by some technicians during the daytime. It was sort of natural for me to return there when I was released. I had a cheap little suitcase with all my earthly belongings.

The lowest point of all happened when I worked for the brewery. They had a donkey, a very dumb donkey, and it ran away. This area north of Munich is very flat and there are fairly deep canals. Well, the dumb donkey fell into one of these canals and I was sent out to retrieve him. All my coaxing was to no avail, the donkey wanted to stay put. The water was filthy brown and smelly. Finally I got him out and dragged him behind me down the village street. The villagers came out and laughed at me. I didn't share their mirth.

My father started a practice in the east even before the war ended. He had a large refugee camp of 5,000 people with cholera and typhus, and they were dying like flies. He took over the camp and stayed in the town. He could have gone to the West; I don't know why he didn't. I guess he thought he had to take care of the people.

My parents stayed in Güstrow-Mecklenburg, a nice middle-sized East German town of 35,000. It was very pleasant with two lakes and a large old castle. I had flown there because it was fifty miles from Warnemünde, where I was in my first flight school. Student pilots made round trip cross-country flights to other airports in the area so I had flown to and from this town's airport in the past.

My father practiced another fifteen years there and he and my mother died within three days of each other, my mother from pancreatic cancer. Now we know this condition is often connected with smoking, the same as bladder cancer. She was in a coma in a hospital with her pancreatic cancer and my father went to church on Sunday and died from a coronary in church like a good Catholic. Both were buried together on September 16. I saw the grave once but now we've given it up. After twenty-five years, graves were taken over by the East German government. We couldn't maintain it; I was in America, my brother was in West Germany, my sister—the youngest—remained in East Berlin.

My brother, Lothar, had also survived the war and was in Budapest. He had been a lieutenant in a Panzer division and may well have survived thanks to Albert Speer, who, at that time, collected 10,000 young German officers to keep them alive—so many men had been killed. Lothar finished high school in 1946, studied medicine in Frankfurt and practiced in Bremerhaven. He died in 1998.

My sister, Christa Fox, studied music and history and worked thirty years for the East German music organization—there was only one organization—they did all the concerts, all the discs, all the tapes—no competition. And so she worked in that central office and never moved very far up in her job. She could have, would have, but she had two brothers in the West, one in America and one in West Germany, and that was an absolute hindrance to her promotion. She was always suspected of having connections to the West. But she didn't suffer; she was a little phlegmatic anyway, so the inconveniences and harassment didn't bother her too much.

When she retired, she was allowed to leave the country one time. We sent her a ticket and she visited us in Fairfield, Virginia, and went back. The East German authorities had hoped she wouldn't come back so they wouldn't have had to pay her social security. When the wall fell, she was free to travel and visit my brother. She now lives in a nice, new, comfortable apartment in Berlin.

Here again, you get into the East German, West German thing and the psychology of all this. It's very interesting. People who lived fifty years under that kind of regime are different; there is no way around it. Whether you were for that regime or against it, just living there for fifty years means that your feelings about other people and the government were bound to be different.

They have had difficulty adjusting to the West German style which is, what shall I say, a little more reckless and closer to the American way of life and doing business and going and pushing and competition and success and money. They had no unemployed people under the old regime and now, suddenly, ten years after reunification, twenty percent of the East German population are still unemployed. In West Germany, it's nine percent. East German wages are a little lower and there are a lot of other problems.

REBUILDING A LIFE

DR. FOX (*continued*). After the Potsdam Agreement and the establishment of East and West Germany, only children of "workers" could study in East Germany. My sister, being the daughter of a "worker-physician" in a communist country, could study. Paradoxically, she went from a Nazi high school in Marienburg in 1944 to a communist school in East Germany and graduated a year later. That was fairly simple; you just had to change things 180 degrees. First, you talk for the Nazis, then you talk against them. Both were absolute systems and there was only one kind of thinking and talking allowed. The mental transition was not as difficult as it would have been if she had had to turn only forty or fifty degrees! I worked on the farm until March 1946. I was hoping the University of Munich would take me because my girlfriend of several years—who later would become my wife—lived there. I heard by word of mouth, however, that Würzburg was available.

I started hitch-hiking because the trains were so crowded. I went to Würzburg and I still had my card designating me as a medical student, but no other papers of any kind. The card was very small like a driver's license, but, with it, I was able to enroll at the University of Würzburg in ten minutes. Then I moved there. I could support myself because my military allotment had accumulated in a bank and my total tuition was only 150 marks per semester, which was the cost of a bottle of wine. So, for a bottle of wine, you could study for half a year.

When I was in Würzburg in medical school, I lived with an old retired railroad couple. He was very dumb and she was not a nice person, but I had a nice room with a view of the Main River. I lived there two and a half years barely surviving. I had kitchen privileges, and one day the wife offered me some soup which was highly unusual. She said, "Molly (the dog) won't eat it!" I could see where I stood.

After four semesters, I took my first medical exam, called the *physicum*, which included the basic sciences—chemistry, physics, biology, physiology, and anatomy. Thank God the exam was behind me when Minister Ludwig Erhard introduced new currency on June 20, 1948. Every German had forty marks, the equivalent of $10. It was a mild catastrophe because suddenly you had no bank account. The forty marks lasted one week—my room was thirty-five marks a week—so there was no choice. I had to start working somehow. Luckily I was living in a village where plums and peaches were grown commercially and I picked all kinds of fruit for three months.

A friend and I had been in medical school together and although I missed classes during this period, her father, a physician, kept her in school and she took meticulous notes which helped me keep up. I got by very well—I didn't miss anything.

Then an interesting thing happened. A dumb (sic) person wanted to change from Munich University to Würzburg University and I wanted to change from Würzburg to Munich. My girlfriend, Trudy, did not continue in medical school when her father was thrown out of office, and she taught public school in Munich. So I traded places with the other student. It was a big and wonderful change.

CHRIS FOX. My mom was a school teacher at the time and she was in a very select group of Fulbright scholars. This was part of a program to sort of brainwash young professionals in Germany so they brought teachers and professionals over to show them the American way—she was one of only six out of a field of 3,000 who were selected. It was extremely selective. So she studied at Peabody College, which is the female part of Vanderbilt University in Nashville, and traveled around the states studying American school systems. She spoke some English, which was not all that common in those days.

DR. FOX (continued). As good as it was, everything was very bureaucratic. For example, to move from one university to another, you had not only had to change your enrollment, but you had to demonstrate that housing at the new university would be available for you as well.

The University of Munich was a little larger and it had a student job referral service through which you could find part-time work that suited you. Through this agency, I worked 4,000 hours in the next two and a half years and I did everything from beating carpets to cleaning parquet floors with steel wool.

I sold things and collected bills for the Bavarian Pharmacy Chamber each month. This gave me enough for my room and to live frugally.

I had one blue suit I left hanging in the Pharmacy Chamber office and I put it on to take my next big exam on thirteen different subjects. I received top marks in all but one subject.

FRAZER. Had you taken any internship?

DR. FOX. The internship was in the first year out of medical school, after taking thirteen subjects with exams. In Germany, the "doctor" title comes before your name, and you are not allowed to use it until you write a dissertation, which I did in three months in 1950. My dissertation title was "Tuberculosis in Pregnant Women." The purpose was to examine pre-and post-natal complications in mothers with TB and problems in their babies after birth. My research was based on about 4,000 births over a twenty-year period— lots and lots of data. Anyway, I was "Doctor" Fox from that point on, and I graduated from the University in 1951.

Then fortuitously, something very nice happened. An old friend of my father came to Munich and hired me as a surgical assistant in a small hospital. At that point, it was probably the most modern small hospital in Europe because the main Volkswagen plant was nearby, and its management wanted the best treatment for its employees. There were 230 beds and each room had its own little terrace; it was really very romantic. I worked there for two and a half years.

"If we really want to love we must learn how to forgive."

MOTHER TERESA

MARRIAGE AND OFF TO AMERICA

CHRIS FOX. Mom and Dad were married in 1954 and, after they pondered the future, Mom said, "Let's go to the States—let's emigrate" and Dad said, "Let's do it." But they needed a sponsor. Mom loved the States and she was a very charming, outgoing person—people were drawn to her. So their sponsor turned out to be Mitchell Dreese, Dean of George Washington University. He had somehow met my mom, I believe it was during the Fulbright interview process, which was somehow involved with the post-war Marshall Plan. Professor Dreese and his wife were very close to my family. In fact, I called him Grandfather Dreese.

My parents came over on a ship that left from Genoa, Italy. Ellis Island was closed a year before they showed up in Newark, New Jersey, and came down to the District of Columbia (DC). My father got a job with the DC General Hospital. He did a lot of ambulance work there and knew every street in the district. He had a great capacity for remembering things, especially how to get to and from all kinds of places. I guess it was the old navigator in him.

FRAZER. How did your medical training and experience mesh with state and federal regulations in America?

DR. FOX. I served two years of a surgical residency before I immigrated to America, but I needed three years' experience in approved American hospitals. The first year was an internship, which I served in the Emergency Hospital in Washington, D.C., and then two years in a residency program in Doctors Hospital in Coral Gables, Florida. You had to have this experience before you could take medical board exams in States like Virginia.

My brother almost caught up with me: He finished medical school as an internist just one semester behind me. He worked most of his life in Bremerhaven up on the coast, but he was with us in Miami in 1956 and 1957. He did an internship in a Catholic hospital in Coral Gables while I was at Doctor's Hospital in the same city.

It was there that I studied for my exams for my Virginia state boards which came in two parts: the basic science segment and the clinical part. I found these harder than the German exams. I had never taken a multiple-choice exam, and I well remember we had sixty minutes to answer 100 anatomy questions. Only about thirty percent of foreign applicants pass the first time, and I did. The language was a problem, but the multiple choice questions were the stuff of nightmares.

I decided not to return to Washington to practice surgery. Conditions for a German doctor in Washington in 1956 were quite different than they are now. There was still a certain antipathy, and I wasn't that wild about surgery even though I knew I was good. Surgeons need referrals; other doctors have to send you patients. Also, I had ample opportunity to observe my father as a general practitioner and the prospect of that kind of career appealed to me.

The Virginia Counsel on Health and Medical Care provided a list of more than fifty available practices state-wide. So we started looking around and it was interesting; this was 1957 and the Brown against the School Board decision was in 1954. There was still some segregation in practices south of Richmond where they had separate waiting rooms for blacks, we knew that was not the future.

We finally found this little office in Fairfield in the Shenandoah Valley. We had wanted to go toward the mountains anyway, and the landscape was beautiful. The office was brand new. About a dozen people in the community had put up $1,000 each to build it. They had a young American doctor there for a year and a half and he couldn't make a go of it and he just left one night. The townspeople were afraid they wouldn't find anybody to take his place, so they were very accommodating. I practiced there from December 15, 1957 until January 15, 1986.

The kindness of the people allowed me to purchase the office in a very short time. They gave me a two-percent, fifteen-year mortgage. The head of Fairfield Enterprise, which built the office, was the president of the local one-room bank and I was able to diagnose a ruptured abdominal aneurysm quickly enough to get him over to Charlottesville. He was a good man and we were friends until he died in his nineties.

My oldest daughter Kathy was born in Florida in 1957, so she is forty-three. She went to Swarthmore College, won a Fulbright Scholarship, studied a year and a half in Hamburg, where she met her Austrian husband-to-be, and eventually got a master's degree at NYU in art history. They now live in Austria and have three children.

My son Christian, now forty-one, was born in Lexington, Virginia. He is a Bates College alumnus and won a one-year scholarship from Rotary Club International, studied a year in Innsbruck and graduated with a degree in geology. He is very senior manager with Baker-Hughes, stationed in London, England. Christian has two boys, Timothy, twelve, and William, ten.

My youngest child, Susi, was also born in Lexington in 1961, went to Dartmouth College, graduated in 1983, and won the only Fulbright awarded that year at Dartmouth. After she finished her Fulbright studies in Europe, she went to the Monterey Language School in California [formerly run by the Army] and received her master's degree in German and French. Then she worked for seven years as an interpreter for the United States Department of State. She is currently in Salzburg conducting major seminars.

All three kids studied German in boarding school, but the girls had an advantage: They spent their fifth grade, ages ten to eleven, with their grandmother in Munich and went to school there for a year. When they came back, they spoke German. Then they took German in college and studied with their Fulbright scholarships in Germany, so they speak the language without an accent. They are absolutely bilingual. But my son has an accent in German. He never had the year as a kid in Germany, and that makes a big difference.

We settled in an old stone house in the middle of the village, with our first daughter. The obstetrician who delivered her in Miami was, in that year, president of the American Obstetrical Society and his name was Fox!

CHRIS FOX. My memory of my dad is that he was one of the hardest workers I knew or had even heard of. He headed off to the hospital in the early morning to make his rounds and came back to his practice, from 10:00 to 2:00. There were a lot of barter payments because it wasn't, and still isn't, a very affluent area. He was also a dispensing physician so he saved patients a lot of hassle because it was a long way to pharmacies. He would go on house calls and he liked it when I rode around with him after school. He used to have some sort of sports car and loved to drive on country roads to treat patients, like old people who did not have transport. He did this every weekday and had evening hours as well for farmers who couldn't make it into town in the daytime.

WHO REMEMBERS WHAT
ABOUT DR. KURT FOX?

AUTHOR'S NOTE. What one of Dr. Fox's long-term employees, a couple of his patients, a close friend and neighbor who lived "just a hill away" from the Fox family recall:

NORMA CULLEN, EMPLOYEE. I was a sheltered little eighteen-year-old when he hired me and took me under his wing. Bit by bit, he trained me to do practically everything RNs (registered nurses) do now. Comforting patients was an important part of my job. This often meant holding a limb Dr. Fox was suturing or what-have-you. I worked for him for twelve years.

Anytime the office was open, it was first come, first served, but I developed an instinct for identifying truly sick patients, and he'd have me call them to his attention and take them first.

Most patients were sick but not traumatized. However, there was no EMS (emergency medical services) at the time, and seriously injured people wound up at our office. One of these was a man whose arm had been all but completely severed just below the elbow. It was just hanging by a tendon. KF (Kurt Fox) had me wrap the arm in a towel and we followed the ambulance to the hospital, where he and a fellow surgeon re-attached the arm so it was apparently fully functional for the rest of the man's life!

If he knew a family had difficult financial problems, he'd take token gifts instead of payments. He gave his life to serving other people, and I wouldn't trade my time and experience with him for anything.

IRENE BRADLEY, PATIENT. When Dr. Fox started practicing in Fairfield he made house calls. My family lived about twenty-five miles from Fairfield, where his office was located. Our house was on the top of a hill about three-quarters of a mile from the main road. The driveway was snow-covered and impassible for cars and my kids had measles, and I'll never forget the sight of Dr. Fox trudging through the snow on foot to treat my kids. He'd do this kind of thing again and again.

His wife Trudy taught German to young students. They were so nice and caring I don't think you could find anyone in Fairfield who didn't love them.

CONNIE GROAH, PATIENT. Dr. Fox delivered two of my children, one of whom, a son, had severe asthma. He didn't require appointments. Patients saw him on a first come, first served basis and his waiting room was always full. His nurse knew the boy's asthmatic condition was serious and always moved him and me to the head of the line.

When one of the boys he delivered graduated from high school, Dr. Fox attended the ceremony. He attempted to do this as often as possible.

He was dearly loved, but he always said what he believed whether people liked it or not.

AUTHOR'S NOTE. The foregoing testimonials speak for themselves and, logistics permitting, I'm sure I could have obtained many more like them. But these perspectives are from people whose relationships with Dr. Fox were primarily professional: Doctor to employee or doctor to patient. Oh, I have had numerous discussions with his very helpful son, Chris, that have yielded other, family, perspectives. But Chris urged me to meet with Paul Wilson, his father's near-contemporary, neighbor and certainly one of the Foxes' best friends. My meeting and subsequent communications with Paul supports information from other sources.

PAUL WILSON. Dr. Kurt Fox ("Kurt") lived and practiced family medicine in Fairfield, Virginia, from August 1957 to March 1986.

My wife Bonny and I were close friends of Kurt and his wife Trudy. We lived "a hill away" from the Foxes from the time they moved to Fairfield in 1976 and often mixed socially with the family.

For thirty years, Kurt served his community like the country doctor depicted by Norman Rockwell. He remembered every ailment of every child, made house calls at all hours, and was authorized to dispense drugs so patients could leave with the pills they needed, rather than having to travel a long distance to a pharmacy, and his fees were astonishingly low. If he saw a facial mole that should come off, he removed it immediately with such precision that no scar was left. His patients recognized their extraordinary good fortune in having "Dr. Fox" (to his patients never "Kurt") as their doctor. He was deeply respected and admired.

He was a very complex human being. He was brilliant and utterly dedicated to providing the best care possible for his patients, but some said overbearing, even a bit authoritative. Patients who ignored his advice were given a fierce scolding. "You are too fat!" he told one of them. "You will die if you don't eat less!" Such directness sometimes shocked patients, but if they were careless of their health, they knew he wasn't. As their doctor, his role was to keep them healthy, and he would do what it took (even offending them) to promote their well-being. He had little time for patients who didn't follow his instructions.

His fellow practitioners recognized Kurt's skill as a diagnostician and surgeon and accorded him considerable respect. He was an innovator and leader in local and medical communities, but some thought he was a bit dogmatic.

Trudy lent balance. She and daughters Kathy and Susi had all been awarded Fulbright scholarships. Her many friends felt Trudy was self-effacing but knew she was always willing to help others. She was the "cruise director" of the family and frequently entertained people new to the area.

Kurt was not a pacifist per se, but he was very much against the Vietnam conflict and opposed to most things military. His feelings in this regard were undoubtedly reinforced by his former German countrymen. Even now, nearly three-quarters of a century after the end of WWII, an overwhelming majority of Germans oppose military action. Chancellor Merkel cannot obtain approval for foreign deployment of German troops, despite huge pressure from her NATO allies, although Germany has been a key member of NATO since its formation.

MAKING THE MOST OF FAMILY TIME

DR. FOX. I functioned as a typical country doctor but also practiced twenty years of obstetrics, admitting patients to Staunton and Lexington, twenty and thirty miles away, respectively. Staunton was where I met the hospital's only full-time obstetrician, Dr. Erskine Sproul. We were in the doctor's lounge one night waiting for our patients to deliver and he asked me an important question, "Didn't you fly?" I said, "Yes," and he asked, "What did you fly?" I said, "Bombers," and he said, "I did too, and I got shot down over Vienna." He had flown a B-17 from Italy to Vienna and wound up spending half a year in a German prison camp. He asked me if I was flying currently and I said, "No." He invited me to join a flying club he belonged to, which had several Cessna light aircraft.

I had to obtain federal and state pilots licenses, but the authorities were very nice about taking into consideration my military experience. I had one logbook from my days flying small airplanes and they said, "That's plenty of flying; you don't have to take the usual fifty hours training, but you have to pass a test." So, I started studying, and what with my obstetrical practice and all, it was just too much—I'd finish the weather book, then the navigation book, and I'd forgotten the first one. Also, I was used to the metric system and everything was different: the degrees, the miles, altitudes, everything.

I finally took a long weekend and studied in a little hut at the Waynesboro Airport. There was a worn-out easy chair and I can still feel the springs on my rear. I spent four days there and, at 2 A.M. on the fourth day, went to the Charlottesville FAA tower and asked to take the exam. The FAA had a safe, and a tower-operator pulled out papers and locked me in a room. Every hour he knocked on the door to see if I wanted to go to the bathroom! So, from 2:00 to 6:00 A.M., I took my exam and passed.

Then I took a test flight with an elderly inspector; he must have been eighty years old (he had flown Junkers in the 1920s). We made a few turns and he said, "You can fly. Let's go back."

Then I flew for about fifteen years—Cessna 150s at $6.00 an hour compared to $50 or so now. We also had Cessna 172s and 182s. I used to fly my wife and three children all over the place. The Cape Hatteras Light House had a strip very close to water's edge and we picnicked on the beach. No tower, no gas, and seldom another plane—it was wonderful.

We flew to Expo '67 in Montreal and a few times to Florida. Then there was a memorable trip to Palm Island. This little island, with its one-way strip, is just north of Hilton Head, South Carolina, and I started my descent about three miles out from 9,000 feet. I was so preoccupied with the

Fox children and mother Trudy with Cessna 172 flown by Kurt Fox. *From left to right:* Chris, Trudy, Susi and Kathy

beauty all around me I neglected the basics: I ran out of gas. This would have been bad enough under any circumstances, but this time I had my mother-in-law aboard! Thank God she never noticed!

CHRIS FOX. I flew with Dad in airplanes belonging to his "Physicians Flying Club," but I didn't have much interest in aviation. But Dad flew the family all over the place. For example, we flew to Expo '67 in Montreal and to Billy Mitchell's WWII strips on the Outer Banks. There were no buildings, and we went swimming. We'd have a picnic under the shade of the wing and fly back up in the evening.

I got airsick in small planes when I was a little kid so when I was about ten, Dad would pile up telephone books or anything that would lift me up so I could fly and I flew all the way—this kept me from getting sick. I'd just keep it level and straight and Dad told me what compass heading to fly. I don't think he was really disappointed that I didn't want to fly; he just wanted me to try it.

DR. FOX (continued). The main reason I kept flying was to transport my family. But as the children grew older and went away to college in the north, bad weather frequently prevented us from flying these little planes to visit them. By then I was sixty and felt it was prudent to have a co-pilot because heart attacks and strokes happen, and I didn't want to put my family at risk, so I dropped out of the club.

I referred many of my patients who needed surgery to Lexington Hospital and often assisted with operations. There is a requirement that, for certain kinds of operations, there must be a second surgeon in case the lead surgeon is incapacitated. I had good surgical training and there were no other surgeons in the area so it was a good arrangement for everybody.

CHRIS FOX. Dad became a very important part of the community. He did everything from house calls—he delivered more than a thousand babies—to many kinds of surgery. Growing up in Nazi Germany gave him a great perspective about what it means to be a good person and what it means to not be one. He wound up being a very active civil rights leader. Fairfield was very southern—still is—there were separate facilities, including the office he took over, and he soon changed that. This was a very important part of who he was. He was a very devoted Democrat. My mom had more time to devote to politics and she was one of the area's leading Democratic Party organizers and was a delegate to the National Convention in 1974.

In 1976, the Carter White House invited my parents to a state dinner honoring Helmut Schmidt. They were seated at a table with Hank Aaron and Secretary of Defense Harold Brown. Dad's comment was, "Wow, you come to America with $400 and a trunk full of clothes and twenty-five years later you're at a dinner at the White House; it could happen only in America." He was certainly proud of his German heritage but he was an extremely proud and committed American.

JULIE FOX (Chris's wife). We keep a notebook wherever we go—little things seem interesting and amusing. It's very rural here and we go to things like the Fireman's Barbecue. Everybody at such events has something interesting to say about Chris's father. For example, we ran across a woman at a fireman's ball who said she was having a long and difficult labor and the baby just wouldn't come out . . . Dad kept insisting she push and push and finally "Dr. Fox made her so mad, her baby just popped out!"

Then I met a seamstress whose several kids had measles. Dr. Fox couldn't get up their long road to their house because of snow in the driveway so he walked a good distance in deep snow to treat the kids in their home. Another time men were trimming Pop's trees and, when his wife asked him about it, he said, "Oh, that was an appendectomy." Sometimes we'd find a pie at the doorstep from someone who couldn't pay a usual fee. He collected 100 per cent of his fees, but quite often in kind rather than cash.

BIG NEEDS, DIFFERENT
KINDS OF PRACTICES

FRAZER. You mentioned that you volunteered to provide medical care for native Americans. Details, please.

DR. FOX. In 1993, I volunteered as a general practitioner for half a year with the Indian Health Service in a Sioux reservation in South Dakota and again for the Owyhee reservation in Nevada in 1996.

I was joined by a surgeon from Puerto Rico whose specialty was hand surgery. Soon after he arrived, twin obese Indian women presented with acute gall bladder problems. They had white counts of 20,000 and the hand surgeon was, well, a bit apprehensive. But I told him I'd help and we started the procedures. The nurses looked at him, they looked at me, and then the instruments, and back at him; they too were apprehensive and you could see it in their eyes. Well, the anesthetist put the first one under and we started out. It soon became evident he didn't know how to do this operation—

you have to practice one or two to pass your surgery boards, but, in his case, it must have been long ago and far away!

All went reasonably well and, when we washed up, he asked me how many of these I had done, and I said I had performed or assisted in quite a few. I knew what to do and what not to do. The most difficult part of the experience was that he didn't speak or understand much English, so we had to improvise and use sign language as we went along. After we did the second twin, this "hand man" was pretty exhausted and he had to sit down and rest.

When I was practicing in Fairfield, many of my patients who needed surgery knew I assisted Dr. Sabastian at Lexington Hospital, and they wanted to go where I was. Most family doctors remain involved anyway, because they want to monitor their patients during and following surgery.

If you are involved with the surgery as well, it makes the patient more comfortable. In any case, I was certainly able to maintain my surgical skills. Then, too, there were elements of surgery in my obstetrical practice which I maintained for twenty years until a specialist moved into the area. Dr. Shields, the surgeon at the Staunton hospital, was a very competent man, and some of my patients would choose to go there. I had to let them decide; if I said, "Don't go to Staunton," they'd probably go anyway and they might not have come back to me.

Along the way, I became the physician in two prisons. The one in Staunton, thirty miles north, was Virginia's geriatric prison. I also became the physician at a nursing home in Clifton Forge, thirty miles west of where I lived. We had thirty-five doctors in the area and nobody wanted to take over nursing homes, so for nine years I had around 125 very old, very sick patients. My other prison was a "road camp" prison with 150 inmates in Greenville, between Fairfield and Staunton. This was a low-security prison that didn't even have a fence around it. Most of the prisoners get paroled before they stayed long, so not many risked the chance of escaping, being caught, and given longer terms.

It's interesting to reflect on the ways I became involved with these facilities. The prison doctor at Greenville, Dr. Thomas, had been there all his life until he retired at eighty-five. State officials found it difficult to find a replacement so they came to me and said, "Oh God, we'll have to close the jail without him." So I said, "All right, I'll do it." And I did—for fifteen years.

The same thing happened in Staunton. There were thirty-five doctors in the city but nobody wanted the jail, so a delegation, headed by the chief doctor from Richmond, came and twisted my arm.

My fast sport cars got me from one location to another, and I was fortunate most of the state troopers were my patients. Nevertheless, when I reached sixty-four, I had to cut back. So, they had built a high-security prison in Craigsville in Augusta County, at the edge of the mountains, west of Staunton. It had lain dormant for two years, but they had to open it to accommodate the burgeoning prison population. So, the officials came with yet another delegation, almost crying. I had a bit of an advantage with them, and I saw my escape route. I pushed them a bit on the salary and suddenly had a forty-hour week, three weeks' vacation, life- and medical insurance, and, best of all, a state pension in five years.

I knew Lexington Hospital wanted to buy my Fairfield office because the administrator had asked me to let him know if I ever wanted to sell it. Lexington wanted to install a doctor who would refer patients to Lexington. Within a week, I had sold my office, finished my practice, and gotten rid of two prisons—all for agreeing to take over the one big prison. But I couldn't get rid of my nursing home responsibilities. It was the same situation; none of the thirty-five doctors in the area wanted to take it over. So, I fulfilled my contract for the remainder of the year and, in January 1986, I became the physician at the high-security correctional facility at Craigsville, Virginia.

I had so much experience with prisoners that I was comfortable with the assignment. It is difficult though, and I would not recommend that a neophyte start in a maximum-security prison. Most of the prisoners in this kind of prison have been in other, less secure jails and prisons at least five or six times. Before I finished in five years, I probably knew more than half the prisoners in Virginia because they rotate.

FRAZER. Did you like some of them?

DR. FOX. No, I can't honestly say that I did. Some of them try to be nice to you, but they are con men through and through. Nevertheless, I think I was considered fair. Guards always brought the prisoners to the clinic and remained while I treated them. It wasn't unusual for a prisoner to stand still, eying me, and say, "You goddamned, mother f . . . g, German bastard." That's your morning greeting, but you just sit still and try your best to not let it get to you—you certainly can't say what's really on your mind. If you did, you'd lose your job, your pension, and whatever.

In thirty years of practice, and twenty years of obstetrics, I never had even the threat of a lawsuit, which in America is unusual. However, I had thirty-five lawsuits alleging malpractice in the five years I was with the jail. Some of the prisoners are "prison lawyers," and they are quite smart, especially when it comes to conjuring up accusations. None of these phony accusations ever came to anything. The last one though was nothing less than ludicrous. I had one prisoner on each of two parallel examining tables. One was a white prisoner with an infected big toe nail which was dirty and stinking and I told him I'd take it off. So, I anaesthetized the toe and took the toenail off. A black man had been sitting on the other table and I told him he'd better not look because it might make him sick. When he started to back talk, I said, "Oh, just keep your mouth shut and sit there."

After I cleaned and dressed the first man's toe, I let him go. Then the black man said, "Doc, you have to take my toe nail off, too." I said, "I'm not going to take your toe nail off, you're in here for a cold." He said, "Well, I have a bad toe nail too," and I told him I'd take a look if he took his shoe off. Now, at this time, it was the fad in this prison for the inmates to wear fancy athletic shoes because the prison was said to have the best basketball court of its kind in Virginia. Most of them have money from drug dealing, and the $150 pair of shoes this man had bought were clearly too small. His toe looked a little tender, but I told him he'd just have to buy a larger pair of shoes. There was no way I was going to take his toenail off and I told him so, and the guard took him away. Two days later, this prisoner sent me a long legal complaint as a preliminary to a lawsuit under federal, not state, law. It alleged bias and a violation of his civil rights because I wouldn't remove the toe nail! State law made no provision for this kind of absurdity, but federal law did and this man found it. Of course, it never came to anything, but it illustrates how enterprising some prisoners are and how careful prison employees must be.

FORGIVENESS, RECONCILIATION
AND ASSIMILATION

AUTHOR'S NOTE. At the beginning of this book, I recounted how Kurt Fox, then a Luftwaffe bomber pilot, sank the USS Maddox (DD-622) carrying 210 Americans to the bottom and leaving seventy-four survivors in WWII. I pondered what enabled these original mortal enemies to forgive and be forgiven? Was it simply the passing of time? Similar or differing cultures? Spirituality? I said only the story of Kurt's life, coupled with observations of those who knew him best, would tell the full story. Now we know a good bit about this amazing man and his brilliant adaptations as he overcame one obstacle after another.

There was one lingering problem, however; even though he didn't see the USS Maddox in its death throes, he knew in his heart of hearts that his bombs had sent it to the bottom. As he thought, "It [the result] had to have been severe and haunted me for much of my life." It may have haunted the survivors on the receiving end equally.

Then came what I call a "God thing." Dr. Fox had retired from full time practice nine years prior to the "unexpected call" he received on January 15, 1995, from Brian Lindner, the historian of the National Life Group in Montpelier, Vermont. Here's the back story:

BRIAN LINDNER. In 1993, National Life wanted to host a ceremony to honor employees who had served in the armed forces. When I started the necessary research someone pointed at a wall in our cafeteria and said: "We used to have plaques honoring our WWI and WWII employees right here." There were holes in the walls but the plaques were gone, and nobody seemed to know what happened to them.

AUTHOR'S NOTE. Brian Lindner, the historian for National Life Group was the prime mover in locating "the German Ju 88 pilot who sank the USS Maddox." This of course turned out to be Dr. Fox, and Brian also arranged to have Dr. Fox meet Maddox survivors.

BRIAN LINDNER (*continued*). I found out that, during the Vietnam conflict, with all the anti-war sentiments, someone said, "We can't have anything that glorifies the military in our building." It seemed probable these big, beautiful plaques had probably been thrown in the dumpster. Well, a company electrician with a lot of longevity found them and took them to one of our outbuildings in an old cow barn. And that's where they sat from sometime in the seventies until 1993. When I pulled the plaques out of a pile in that barn I saw one name with a star on it and it said, "Ensign Robert Crathorne, killed in action, USS Maddox, (DD-622)." So I thought, wow, here's something I'll really look into (I have

Brian Lindner prior to the Maddox Survivors' meeting. Courtesy of National Life Group

researched all the guys from my hometown who were killed in action, so I had good experience in doing this).

I found out there was an organization called "The Maddox Association." So I contacted them and found they had a reunion in Portland, Maine, and I went to that event. While talking with some of the survivors I said, "Wouldn't it be

neat if we could find the German crew that sunk you guys."
Several members said, "Well, you find that crew and we'll
invite them to a reunion," and I accepted the challenge.

I had exchanged research with a German historian in the
past. I told him all the things we knew. We knew it was
a Junkers 88, we knew the date, we knew the place, and I
asked him if he could find the crew.

It took him several months before he called back to say, "I
found them!" And he added, "By the way, the pilot lives in
America," and that he found the radio operator as well. He
found this information through veterans' organizations in
Germany.

So then I called Dr. Fox one evening at about dinner time.
At first, he was very standoffish but, after an hour or so, he
said, "Well, yeah, it probably was my crew." And from that
point forward, we developed a relationship and he under-
stood we weren't out to publicize him as a "Nazi pilot," or
any such foolishness.

DR. FOX'S WRITE-UP ABOUT THE THOMASVILLE REUNION. The
surprise call I received on January 15, 1995, was from Brian
Lindner, of National Life Group in Vermont. Although I had
been in contact with a couple of my former Ju 88 crewmembers, this was the first time I heard that Maddox survivors
got together every year and circulated a biannual newsletter.
Mr. Lindner is an amateur military historian and he came
across information about the Maddox sinking when he was
searching for names of his company's employees who were
killed in WWII.

Pat Sykes, a Maddox survivor, read an article in his organization's house organ which referred to reunions held by
former Navy shipmates. He located a reunion of his former

crewmates and attended his first Maddox reunion in June, 1994. It was here that Sykes learned National Life Group had hosted the fiftieth anniversary of the Maddox sinking in 1993, to especially pay tribute to Ensign A. Robert Crathorne, Jr., a former National Life employee who went down with the ship.

Lindner and Sykes became intrigued with the idea of finding the pilot of the plane that bombed the Maddox.

Here in America and abroad, there are private military historians and they often work with one another. As it happened, the Vermont historian knew an amateur historian in Germany for whom he had once done a favor. So when his American friend and fellow historian asked him to help, he said he'd try. It was an easy matter for him to determine which German units had bombers in the vicinity on the day of the sinking.

Most former German Air Force units have their own survivor organizations, ours included, so the researcher contacted our organization to refine his search. He verified the bomber must have come from our unit and our correspondent let it be known that historians were seeking information about a ship bombing on July 10, 1943, at 5:00 A.M. My former radio operator keeps in touch with this group, and he said his diary showed this was exactly the date and time we recorded our hit. He also keeps in touch with me and readily gave them my name and address back here in the States.

I soon received calls in rapid succession from Lindner and Sykes. Sykes asked if he could come up from Thomasville, North Carolina, where his survivor organization is located. With more than a little trepidation, I agreed to the get-together, which proved to be surprisingly relaxed and comfortable for both of us. But the ensuing invitation

Dr. Fox (under arrow) with Maddox Survivors

from Lindner made me a bit anxious: Would I address their annual meeting in Thomasville, North Carolina?

I tentatively agreed providing nobody in the organization had any objections, and then only if I was assured there would not be any media. I guess my anxiety was, at least in part, because I had seen some crying Japanese pilots on TV and it was difficult for all concerned. Well, they met all my conditions so I attended.

The men were very nice and matter-of-fact. Their attitude seemed to be simply, "Well, you shot at us, and we shot at you, you hit us and we missed you, so that's it." After dinner, we all met in the basement of the hall and, after various members described their recollections of the sinking, it was my turn to speak. For me, it was a bit of a ticklish situation.

Most of the members seemed to be churchgoers and, after the second day, we all attended a service in a Baptist church. Many of the members of the congregation who had noth-

Dr. Fox with a Me 262 similar to the jets he flew

ing to do with the sinking came out to see what was going on and, obviously, to have a good look at the man who had wrought so much damage. My feelings of discomfiture were certainly lessened when, after the service, we adjourned for dinner. The break-out room was decorated with American *and* German flags! I managed to say some more or less fitting words, but with a bit of a lump in my throat. It was poignant.

Pat Sykes nominated me to be a member of the Maddox Association. This motion was approved with only a minimum of opposition. Tragically, Pat died from stomach cancer six weeks later.

FRAZER. On September 7, 2001, just four days before 9/11, Dr. Fox was the honored guest of the Delaware Valley Historic Aircraft Association (DVHAA) at the Willow Grove Naval Air Station at Willow Grove, Pennsylvania. A German Me 262 had just been refurbished and presented to the

Two Tuskegee airmen on Dr. Fox's left and right side (back row of picture)

Robert Fischer, a docent at DVHAA, arranged for the Me 262 model Dr. Fox is shown holding in the accompanying picture with Les Querry on the left and Mr. Fischer on the right.

public, which was also treated to a demonstration by the Blue Angels.

The same Me 262 was inducted into the DVHAA three years later, in 2004, and Dr. Fox was again the honored guest. Both meetings were especially notable for two reasons: First, Dr. Fox was thought to have been the only former 262 pilot living in America; and, second, because both meetings included former Tuskegee Airmen, the only Black pilots in WWII. These men distinguished themselves as U.S. Army Air Corps P-51 pilots. In fact, one member of their squadron shot down an Me 262 flown by Dr. Fox!

Dr. Fox died seventeen years later, on September 8, 2012, in his home in Charlottesville, Virginia, at age ninety.

"Without forgiveness, there's no future."

BISHOP DESMOND TUTU

EPILOGUE

The key question is this: What enabled Dr. Fox and the members of the Maddox Survivors Association to forgive and to be forgiven? Was it simply the passing of time? Similar or differing cultures? Spirituality? Assimilation? There are elements of all these attributes and literally thousands more relating to the subject of forgiveness and its corollary, reconciliation.

Hurtful memories fade as time passes, cultures blend as communications improve, and spirituality remains essentially constant. In Dr. Fox's case, assimilation was an important factor; he became a productive, respected American citizen who gave of himself in many ways.

We submit that an important aspect of the question in this, and similar cases are anonymity and its converse, familiarity. Many WWII American crewmembers involved with strategic bombing wiped out entire cities of innocent civilians who were "enemies" and anonymous at the time. After the war, many of the men who toggled the bombs forged life-long friendships with survivors.

Forgiveness is not a consensus; it involves a party of only one. It is a decision we make by ourselves and for ourselves.

As Dr. Fox said: "Meeting the Maddox survivors face-to-face was a truly liberating experience," and the survivors, one-by-one, voted to make him an honorary member of the Maddox Survivor group.

It was extreme forgiveness.